The Landscape of Wessex

J. H. BETTEY

The Landscape of Wessex

Moonraker Press

© 1980 J. H. Bettey
First published in 1980 by MOONRAKER PRESS
26 St Margaret's Street, Bradford-on-Avon, Wiltshire
SBN 239 00197 4 (paperback 239 00242 3)
Printed and bound in England by
Butler & Tanner Ltd, Frome and London

Contents

Acknowledgements

The assistance of many people who have helped by providing information or photographs is gratefully acknowledged. Thanks are due to the archivists of Bristol, Dorset, Somerset and Wiltshire; to the various county archaeological societies; to numerous friends and colleagues, including Anthony Adams, Alan Andrew, Gordon Kelsey and Kenneth Rogers; and to Rosemary Johnston for her secretarial assistance. Many of the subjects discussed and illustrated in the following pages were initially explored with students on courses of the University of Bristol Department of Extra-Mural Studies. The aerial photographs are from the superb collection amassed over many years by Jim Hancock, and the frontispiece photograph by Gerd Franklin. The photograph of Stourhead on the dust jacket is reproduced by permission of the National Trust.

Introduction

This book describes the development of the landscape of the counties of Avon, Dorset, Somerset and Wiltshire, and by means of examples and illustrations shows the ways in which the landscape of the region has been used, changed and fashioned over the centuries. Few areas have a more diverse geology or a greater variety of distinctive scenery than Wessex; it includes the great chalk downlands of Hampshire and Berkshire, Wiltshire and Dorset, the lush and wooded clay vales and pasture lands of north Wiltshire, east Somerset and west Dorset, as well as the marshlands of Somerset, the limestone heights of Mendip and, in the far west, the Quantock, Blackdown and Brendon hills and the majestic sweep of Exmoor. Reflecting this variety of landscape and scenery are the contrasting coastlines of Dorset and Somerset, and the distinctive ports and harbours of the English Channel and the Bristol Channel. A traveller through this region cannot fail to notice the frequent and dramatic changes in scenery; the observant will also notice the different ways in which each landscape has been adapted by human activity, the contrasts in the size, shape and frequency of villages and towns, the varieties of farming practice, the different field-shapes, road patterns and the evidences of former industries. In all parts of the region can be seen the extensive signs of prehistoric settlement and the evidences in the landscape of continuity and of long centuries of human use and adaptation: the dramatic Iron Age hill forts on the downlands, the Roman roads running for miles across the region with few, if any, villages along their length; the nucleated, compact villages of the chalklands, and the contrast they present with the dispersed settlement and scattered farmsteads of parts of the claylands; the small irregular fields of some areas and the large rectangular enclosures in others; the numerous fine churches, often with extravagant towers, in villages which seem far too small ever to have been able to afford to build them; the large numbers of great estates with fine mansions set in wooded parkland; the apparent superfluity of little market towns whose narrow streets and tight bends were clearly never intended to accommodate modern traffic. Everywhere there are the signs of former human use and of the unremitting toil of countless generations. The results of their labours show in hedges, buildings, churches and chapels, ports and harbours, military fortifications, roads, bridges, canals and railways. It is the diversity of landscape which gives the area much of its attraction, and which has resulted in such a varied pattern of landscape development.

The abundant evidence of the continuity of human occupation and use over a very long period of time which can almost everywhere be observed, is the most notable of all the landscape features of the region. This is seen most dramatically in some of the huge areas which have been taken over for military purposes, especially on the chalklands of Wiltshire and on the Dorset heath; all over these tracts of ground now used for military training can be seen the barrows, standing stones, field-systems, abandoned tracks and roads, and other evidence of intensive use by prehistoric communities. The great naval base and underwater research establishment on the island of Portland, with the most sophisticated modern equipment, is surrounded by ancient fields and prehistoric remains; the tank training-grounds and nuclear research plant on the Dorset heath, like the military areas on Salisbury Plain and along the Dorset coast, are in a countryside thickly covered with barrows, hill-forts and other evidences of prehistoric activity; while the planes from the huge naval airfield at Yeovilton take off over the former Roman town of Lindinis. A different example of contrasting and even of conflicting land-use can be observed by travellers along the M4 motorway between Bath and Swindon, where for many miles the fences on either side of the motorway have been expensively adapted to prevent the fox-hounds of the Duke of Beaufort's hunt from coming on to the road.

The basic geological divisions of the region have been the primary cause of the varied development of its landscape; it is the rocks and soils which have been the essential setting for man's activities and which have assisted or discouraged succeeding generations in their work of changing the landscape and creating the modern scenery. The diversity of the region's underlying geology can be observed in its building stones. The Carboniferous Limestone of the Mendip region and the Dolomitic Conglomerate found alongside it can be seen in churches and houses throughout Bristol, south Avon and north Somerset; in the Somerset Lowlands are extensive areas of White and Blue Lias which has frequently been used in buildings in conjunction with the loveliest of all Somerset stones, the golden stone of the Upper Lias from Ham Hill, seen to perfection in such buildings as Montacute House or Sherborne Abbey and in a host of other churches and houses. It is the use of this beautifully coloured and textured Ham Hill stone which makes such church towers as Ile Abbots and Kingsbury Episcopi so memorable. Somerset and south Avon also have fine oolitic limestones which include the stone from Dundry Hill overlooking Bristol, from the famous quarries around Bath, and from the quarries at Doulting near Shepton Mallet which provided the stone for Wells Cathedral and for many other churches including the lovely towers of Chewton Mendip and Evercreech. In the Quantocks the red sandstone has been widely used and is responsible for the strikingly attractive colour of churches such as Bishop's Lydeard, Halse and Crowcombe, and of houses such as Cothelstone and Crowcombe Court. In Wiltshire stone from the great oolite quarries of Corsham and Box has been extensively used in the north and north-west of the county, while in the south Chilmark quarries provided the stone for Salisbury Cathedral and many other buildings. The Wiltshire greensand has also been widely used in building, especially around Potterne and in the south-west of the county from Maiden Bradley to Zeals and Penselwood, and greensand is to be found in buildings throughout much of east Dorset. Most of the chalk is too soft to make good building stone, so that in the chalkland areas of both Wiltshire and Dorset brick building predominates as it does in those parts of west Wiltshire and north Dorset where there is little good building stone, and for less expensively constructed buildings, cob and thatch has been the traditional material. Dorset has two fine stones which have been used all over the country—the stone of Portland and Purbeck. The Purbeck quarries also provided the 'marble' for countless church monuments as well as roofing 'slate' which can be seen on the roofs of houses at Corfe Castle and Worth Matravers as well as in many other villages in that area. In west Dorset the Blue Lias is extensively used in buildings, especially around Bridport and Lyme Regis. As in Wiltshire, brick has been much used throughout the Dorset chalklands, at least from the seventeenth century, and is to be seen in Bloxworth House (1608), the beautifully proportioned Anderson Manor (1622) and in the excellent brick buildings of Poole, Wareham,

1 Cheddar Gorge (Photograph: J. E. Hancock)

2. Battlesbury hill-fort near Warminster and the expanse
of Salisbury Plain (Photograph: J. E. Hancock)

Weymouth, Dorchester and best of all, Blandford Forum, which was largely rebuilt in brick after the disastrous fire of 1731.

It is scarcely possible to find any place in the region where some evidence of man's impact upon the landscape is not to be seen, although a few areas still retain much of their natural vegetation and appearance. The heathlands of east Dorset remain barren and infertile, and the efforts of succeeding generations of farmers have had little effect upon the poor, acid soils. Thomas Hardy's description of this part of Wessex which he called 'Egdon Heath' cannot be bettered:

Civilization was its enemy and ever since the beginning of vegetation its soils had worn the same antique brown dress.

Some of the bleaker and more stony parts of the chalklands also preserve their ancient appearance, especially parts of Fyfield Down and Overton Down near Marlborough; while on Salisbury Plain and along the Dorset coast military occupation has allowed some parts to revert to a natural vegetation of scrub and woodland, notably around the former villages of Imber (Wiltshire) and Tyneham (Dorset) from which the inhabitants were expelled. In a few heavily wooded parts of west Dorset, on the highest slopes of Mendip and across some parts of Exmoor man has had only a limited impact upon the landscape, but almost everywhere else the signs of incessant, prolonged human activity are to be seen. Even in the wildest and most remote areas there is generally some evidence, if only in the form of those silent witnesses to continuity, the prehistoric burial mounds or barrows. Wessex is notable for this wealth of prehistoric survivals in the landscape, especially across those parts of the chalklands which have escaped subsequent interference by the plough, and the surviving evidence for prehistoric land-use must be the starting point for any discussion of landscape development in the region.

The Prehistoric Landscape

The impact of prehistoric settlers and farmers upon the landscape can more easily be appreciated on the chalklands of Wessex than anywhere else in England, while throughout the whole region the part played by the Romans and Saxons in changing the landscape and subduing the forests can still be clearly seen. It is on the chalk downlands that most of the evidence for prehistoric settlement and land-use survives; but recent archaeological work has demonstrated beyond doubt that prehistoric occupation was by no means confined to these high lands, and it is only because this land has not been used intensively again until the mechanised farming of the twentieth century, that so much prehistoric evidence survives there. It is quite clear that prehistoric peoples lived also on the lower lands and in the valleys, but the evidence in these more favoured sites has generally been obliterated by later occupation.

The earliest human inhabitants of the region, the Palaeolithic and Meso-lithic hunters, have left little discernible evidence of their existence upon the landscape, although their flint tools, microliths and a few habitation-sites have been found in the gravel terraces of the rivers Frome and Stour in Dorset, along the Avon near Salisbury and in the caves at Cheddar, Wookey and Westbury-sub-Mendip in Somerset; an important Mesolithic settlement has also been excavated on the island of Portland. It was the Neolithic settlers who first left clear signs of their presence upon the land-scape of Wessex. These were farmers who came into southern England from the continent from about 3500 B.C., bringing with them hitherto un-known techniques of agriculture and stock-breeding. The hill-top cause-wayed enclosure on Windmill Hill near Avebury where their occupation was first recognised has given its name to the culture and life-style of these settlers, and evidences of their influence on the landscape can also be dis-cerned at Knap Hill (Alton Barnes), Whitesheet Hill (Kilmington) in Wilt-shire, or at Maiden Castle and Hambledon Hill in Dorset, beside or be-neath the later Iron Age hill-forts. They also introduced a distinctive and remarkable feature into the landscape of Somerset by the network of wooden trackways, beautifully constructed out of the natural vegetation of hazel and birch wood and other branches, which they laid across the marshy lands in the Somerset levels to form causeways. Over 40 of such Neolithic trackways have been found in the Somerset levels, the finest of them in the area between the Polden Hills and the 'island' of Wedmore. Already some 14 miles of trackway have been discovered, and many more must already have been destroyed by modern peat-digging in the area, or must as yet remain hidden. The marshy ground has not only protected these trackways from decay, but has also preserved both the wood and the minute grains of pollen which have enabled modern scientific techniques of analysis to date them and to estimate the sort of woodland and other vegetation which covered the area between 3000 and 2000 B.C. The trackways are also important because they show the intensive way in which the land was used by Neolithic farmers, and the level of sophistication and organisation in the society that could build these elaborately constructed roads over such difficult terrain. But the most conspicuous survival of Neolithic occupation consists of the long barrows in which they buried their dead, like the famous examples at West Kennet near Avebury, at Pimperne near Blandford Forum, the fine barrow at Stoney Littleton near Bath and others along the line of Mendip and in many other places. The Neolithic people were also responsible for the strange earthwork known as the Dorset 'Cursus' on Cranborne Chase, which consists of two parallel banks running for six and a half miles across country from the Chase almost to Bokerley Dyke—this is one of the great monuments of prehistoric Britain, but there is little agreement as to its purpose. The massive 'henge' monuments which survive as such prominent features of the Wessex landscape are also the work of this period. They include Durrington Walls and the stone circles at Avebury, Marsden and Stanton Drew, as well as the beginning of the complex development of the most celebrated prehistoric monument in Britain, the great sarsen circle at Stonehenge. Three other ritual sites or 'henge' monuments also date from the Neolithic period. They are Maumbury Rings, the impressive earthworks on the out-

3 Avebury, the great bank and ditch enclosing the stone circles
(Photograph: J. E. Hancock)

4 Stonehenge, the best known and most visited prehistoric
monument in the country (Photograph: Geological Museum)

skirts of Dorchester, Mount Pleasant on the other side of Dorchester, and
Knowlton on the road between Cranborne and Wimborne, where the ruins
of Knowlton church now occupy the area inside the rampart. Whatever
the precise meaning and purpose of these impressive sites, it is certain that
people who could undertake the building of such monuments had an extra-
ordinary degree of organisation and a way of life which allowed considerable leisure from the elementary business of obtaining food and shelter.
The fact that the Neolithic settlers were farmers also means that they must
have had a considerable effect on the landscape by clearing scrub and
woodland, by cultivating small patches of ground and by the effect of the
grazing of the goats, sheep, pigs and cattle which they kept.

THE BRONZE AGE
About 2000 B.C. another group of settlers moved in to Wessex, the Bronze
Age people. They continued and extended the farming activities of their
predecessors, but their most prominent and widespread memorials in the
landscape consist of the round barrows in which they buried their dead.
Many hundreds of these round barrows survive right across Wessex, and

13

5 The Westbury White Horse on the escarpment below the Bratton hill-fort, where the clay vale of Wiltshire ends and the chalk downlands of Salisbury Plain begin. The White Horse, one of many such hill figures in Wiltshire, was constructed in the eighteenth century (Photograph: J. E. Hancock)

6 Maumbury Rings on the southern outskirts of Dorchester. Originally a Neolithic henge monument, it was later converted into a Roman amphitheatre. During the Civil War in the seventeenth century it was used as a gun emplacement (Photograph: J. E. Hancock)

7 Silbury Hill, the enormous artificial earthen mound, during floods with the surrounding ditch full of water (Photograph: J. E. Hancock)

can be seen against the skyline of the chalk downlands in many parts of the region as well as on Mendip, the Quantock, Blackdown and Brendon Hills, and on Exmoor. The South Dorset Ridgeway has the largest number of barrows of any area in the country, and the biggest group of all is at Poor Lot, near Winterbourne Abbas, where there are no less than 44 barrows. Many of these have been greatly damaged in recent years by modern ploughing, and for example less than 15 per cent of all the Dorset barrows remain unharmed. The Wessex landscape is especially rich in round barrows; some 6,000 have been recorded and there must have been many more which have been destroyed over the centuries. The obviously planned siting of many of these barrows in straight lines along the skyline or at the top of slight rises of ground presupposes an open unobstructed countryside and downland at about 1500 B.C. Throughout the Bronze Age also the great monument at Stonehenge continued its complicated architectural development. The size, complexity and mystery of monuments such as Avebury, Stonehenge, Stanton Drew and the strange enigma of Silbury Hill, as well as the obvious skill and sophisticated organisation required for their construction, serve to remind us forcibly of the energy of the early inhabitants of Wessex who made the first major modifications to the landscape.

THE IRON AGE

Much more widespread visible evidence survives of the activities of the Iron Age farmers, since not only do their great hill-forts continue to dominate many parts of the region, but their 'Celtic' fields are still very clearly to be seen in many places. Hill-forts are found predominantly in Wales and the south-west, and in Wessex they range from small defensive enclosures of two or more acres with a single bank and ditch, like Spetisbury Rings, to the complex multiple ramparts and ditches enclosing some 47 acres at Maiden Castle, or the great earthworks at Hambledon and Eggardon, at Yarnbury Castle (Berwick St James, Wilts.) or Bratton Castle; in Somerset impressive Iron-Age hill-forts dominate the hill-tops of Ham Hill and South Cadbury, while in Avon are Sodbury and the magnificently situated fort of Dolebury. On the summit of Walbury Hill in Berkshire, 975 ft above sea-level and the highest point on the chalk downs of Wessex, the dramatic hill-fort with a single bank and ditch encloses an area of 82 acres. Nearly 150 hill-forts and similar fortified enclosures have been identified in Wessex; many date from the early Iron Age, though a few like Spetisbury in Dorset and Ladle Hill in Hampshire were still being built at the time of the Roman conquest. Some at least of these hill-forts were permanently occupied, although others may have been built primarily as animal enclosures and were used for defence only during periods of danger. A few like Beacon Hill and Abbotsbury Castle had permanent huts within their ramparts; others like the great forts at Hod Hill, Hambledon and Maiden Castle each had more than 200 circular huts and were clearly the sites of large and important permanent communities.

All the Wessex hill-forts are interesting and worth visiting; two of the grandest and most spectacular are Maiden Castle and Eggardon. Maiden Castle was the largest and most elaborately defended fort of the Durotriges tribe, and its massive ramparts and ditches together with the complicated defences of its entrance are awe-inspiring in their grandeur and complexity. Many of the finds produced by the archaeological excavation of Maiden Castle can be seen in the excellent museum of the Dorset Archaeological Society in nearby Dorchester. Eggardon Hill, ten miles west of Maiden Castle is notable not just for the scale of its defences but also for its spectacular site on the spur of a hill looking out across the lovely west Dorset countryside to the sea.

But the archaeological evidence from the Iron Age is not all of military sites; less impressive but no doubt more characteristic and equally important for the landscape is the evidence of agriculture, trade and industry. The lakeside dwellings of Glastonbury and Meare are probably the survivors of many other similar small settlements which formerly existed in the Somerset marshlands. The enclosures and farmsteads at Woodcuts, Hog Cliff Hill and Pimperne, or Cowdown (Longbridge Deverill), and perhaps most impressive of all, the 'Celtic' fields which are to be found throughout the region, also illustrate the activity of early farmers in the region. These Celtic fields are rectangular or square enclosures, ranging from a quarter of an acre to two acres or more in size, and they are especially numerous and evident on the chalk hillsides where their low hedges show up clearly, especially when the sun is at a low angle. The distinctive shape of the fields, which were used for growing crops, owes its origin to the small wooden plough or 'ard', drawn by small oxen, which was used by Iron Age farmers. This was a primitive and inefficient instrument for it lacked coulter and mould-board and could not therefore turn a furrow; it did little more than scratch a groove through the earth, and it was necessary to plough the land several times in both directions in order to obtain a satisfactory tilth. For such a method of cultivation, called cross-ploughing, rectangular or square fields were obviously the most satisfactory. This type of farming continued throughout the Roman period. Barley was the crop most widely grown during the early Iron Age; a wheat known as *emmer* was also produced, and later this was joined and to some extent supplanted by a new species of wheat called *spelt*. Grain was stored inside wickerwork containers in sealed pits, which are one of the most characteristic features of Iron Age settlements in Wessex. Each pit could be used only for a few years, since it would soon become 'sour' and spoil the grain; many were later filled with domestic rubbish, while a few were used for human burials. Nearly 200 grain storage-pits were found at Little Woodbury, south of Salisbury, where an Iron Age farmstead has been excavated. The circular farmhouse was built of wood, with a thatched roof, and around it were the bell-shaped pits for storing grain, and cob or clay ovens for drying the corn.

Evidence also survives in the landscape of Iron Age pastoral farming. Tracks and droveways for taking cattle to and from their pastures have been found, as well as enclosures obviously designed for livestock. Examples can be seen at Fyfield Down near Marlborough or at Lyscombe Hill near Melcombe Horsey in Dorset. Remains and evidence also survive of Iron Age industries—the making of pottery, the preparation of salt along the Dorset coast and some stone-quarrying including the extraction of shale at Kimmeridge for ornaments. The existence of a metal currency implies a considerable degree of trading as well as a sophisticated political organisation. The fact that so many 'Celtic' fields, barrows, earthworks and other reminders of prehistoric activity survive on the chalklands of Wessex where the archaeological evidence has not been destroyed by later ploughing, and that what does remain is probably only a small fraction of what once existed, is impressive evidence for the intensive use of the prehistoric landscape; it also suggests a sizeable population in the area.

THE ROMANS

The conquest of Wessex was undertaken by the Roman forces soon after their landing at Richborough in the late summer of A.D. 43. The task of subduing the British tribes, the Atrebates and the Durotriges, strongly entrenched behind their massive hill-forts, was given by the Roman commander Aulus Plautius to his most trusted lieutenant, Vespasian (later Emperor), who led the II Augusta Legion. The historical evidence of the campaign rests on the few details given in the biography of Vespasian by Suetonius. This states that in Britain Vespasian 'fought thirty battles, subjugated two warlike tribes and captured more than twenty *oppida* (fortresses) beside the Isle of Wight'. The *oppida* referred to are no doubt the great hill-forts, and it is a measure of the efficiency of the Roman army that these fortifications were overcome with such speed. There is archaeological evidence of the way in which the hill-forts fell before the Roman advance and of the ruthless skill of the Roman army as a fighting machine. The battle cemetery at Spetisbury has yielded impressive confirmation of the slaughter inflicted by the Roman army, testimony of their skill in attack comes from Hod Hill where the defences were stormed after a preliminary bombardment with ballista bolts, and the most dramatic evidence of all comes from Maiden Castle. Here a hastily contrived cemetery containing the graves of 28 native warriors was found at the east gate; many of the mutilated skeletons showed signs of terrible injuries and one still had the head of a Roman ballista bolt fixed in its backbone.

Perhaps nowhere in Wessex is one made more aware of the might of the Roman army than at Maiden Castle, where in spite of the immense fortifications which are still so impressive after nearly 2,000 years, the

Durotriges could in no way match the trained Roman forces.

The impact of the Romans upon the landscape of Wessex during the period from the first to the fifth century was enormous, and is still very evident. The great Roman roads with their intricate system of connecting minor roads and lanes still form the basis of parts of the modern road system, especially the Fosse Way between Bath and Ilchester. The great towns—Bath, Dorchester, Ilchester, Cunetio (near Marlborough)—with their temples and public buildings, baths, aqueducts and ramparts, the commercial centres such as Camerton, Charterhouse-on-Mendip, and the villas and romanised farms which are to be found all over the countryside of Wessex, had as great an effect on the landscape as the presence of the Roman armies had upon the political and economic life of the region. During the centuries of Roman peace, population grew considerably and new land was brought into cultivation, particularly on the chalk downlands. The greatly increased demand for farm produce, especially for corn, to feed the army of occupation and to export to other parts of the Empire, was largely met by increasing production in southern England. It meant that farming was rapidly expanded and the Celtic fields reached their fullest extent. By the second century of Roman rule villas were being established in many places in the region. Known sites are most numerous in the valleys, but it is probable that many others are situated beneath existing villages and remain unrecognised.

Villas which have been excavated contained mosaics of great artistic merit. The fourth-century mosaic pavement from the villa at Hinton St Mary in Dorset is now in the British Museum; it shows the bust of a man with the early christian *chi-rho* monogram behind his head, with other busts in each of the four corners of the pavement; all around are hunting scenes, Bellerophon riding Pegasus, hounds and deer. The bust with the *chi-rho* has been interpreted as a representation of Christ, while the other figures may represent the Evangelists. If this is correct, it is a remarkable early example of the impact of Christianity upon the region. Other mosaics also with the *chi-rho* symbol have been found elsewhere in Dorset. Another fine mosaic pavement comes from Low Ham in Somerset and can now be seen in the Castle Museum at Taunton. This shows scenes based on the story of Dido and Aeneas from Virgil's *Aeneid*. The mosaic floor of a Roman villa at Keynsham is now on show in J. S. Fry's chocolate factory, and depicts the story of Europa being carried off by Jupiter disguised as a bull. These and other mosaics which have been found at villa-sites throughout the region demonstrate both the extent of Roman influence and the wealth and prosperity which came with the four centuries of Roman peace, enabling these fine villas with their expensive floors and elaborate baths to be built.

The visitor to Dorchester should not miss the remarkable Roman house which is situated in the north-west angle of the defences around the Roman

8 Continuity of landscape use on the northern outskirts of Dorchester. In the centre is Poundbury Iron Age hill fort; the industrial area beyond is situated on an important Roman cemetery just outside the walls of the Roman town of Durnovaria to which water was brought by the remarkable aqueduct. Also included in this view are the seventeenth-century water meadows in the Frome valley and the nineteenth-century railway (Photograph: J. E. Hancock)

Durnovaria. The site is now part of the grounds of the County Hall and is open to the public. This is the foundations and part of the walls of the only town-house visible anywhere in Britain. The house included living and sleeping rooms, a bath suite with under-floor heating, and beside it a blacksmith's shop. All the principal rooms had mosaic pavements, although only one is now visible.

The farming associated with the Roman villas was no doubt in advance of the old-established agricultural practices, for the Romans introduced improved ploughs, better facilities for corn-drying and storage, and improved mills. But the older, more primitive agriculture in the native tradition continued to exist; many isolated Romano-British farmsteads have been identified and countless others must be buried beneath later farms and fields. In Wiltshire a good example was excavated at Berwick Down, Tollard Royal, and in Avon a small Romano-British farm at

9 Yarnbury Castle on Salisbury Plain, one of the
most impressive of the Wiltshire hill-forts. Later
the site was used for an annual sheep fair and the
marks made by the pens, booths and standings
at the fair can still be seen (Photograph: J. E.
Hancock)

10 The Iron-Age fort on Hambledon Hill, Dorset,
showing the great defensive ramparts and the evidences of occupation of the interior (Photograph:
J. E. Hancock)

Butcombe has been shown to have consisted merely of a house and byre
or farm building, set in a farmyard containing animal pens and surrounded
by a few small fields enclosed by stone walls. A much larger farm has been
excavated at Catsgore in Somerset; this was situated near the important
Roman town of Ilchester, and the large complex of buildings included
corn-driers, storage-bins, byres and other farm buildings. In the later
Roman period more emphasis seems to have been placed on pastoral farming, perhaps because of an increased demand for locally produced meat
and wool, perhaps because supplies of corn were now becoming available
from the newly drained Fenland of eastern England. The importance of
this pastoral farming has been demonstrated from excavations of villas on
the rich soils round Ilchester—an area admirably adapted for grassland
and grazing.

The Roman impact on the landscape also included the great road system
which will be discussed in more detail in Chapter 7, and Roman temples
at Jordon Hill near Weymouth, Chew Stoke near Bristol, Weycock Hill
(Berkshire) and Nettleton Shrub north-east of Bath. The Romans had a
major effect upon the landscape through their industrial activities—lead-
mining on Mendip, iron-working in parts of Wiltshire, coal-mining in
north Somerset, stone-quarrying in various parts of the region, and the
working of shale from Kimmeridge and elsewhere in the isle of Purbeck
to produce ornaments, decoration and furnishings. Roman pottery kilns

have also been found in many parts of the region, notably around the shores of Poole harbour. At Charterhouse-on-Mendip the remains of a small Roman amphitheatre can still be clearly seen in the fields. This is an oval enclosure with steeply raked sides, constructed by the Roman lead miners who came to Mendip to exploit the lead there soon after the Roman landing, and set up an important industry extending over a wide area of the surrounding hills. Here they produced the lead which was needed in such quantities for pipes and coffins, and for mixing with tin to produce pewter for tableware. The Roman energetic exploitation of the lead resources on Mendip is probably the first example in the region of a large-scale industry concentrated in one place.

Another Roman amphitheatre was created out of the Neolithic earthwork at Maumbury Rings, just outside Dorchester, an impressive site well worth visiting. Here again the visitor is powerfully reminded of the impact which Roman occupation had upon the region. Dorchester also possesses a remarkable example of Roman engineering in the form of an aqueduct designed to bring water to the town of Durnovaria. This is 12 miles in length, and brought a constant supply of water from the river Frome into the town by a carefully constructed channel which follows a circuitous route along the contours of the downland to the north-west of the town.

This fine example of civil engineering is still clearly visible in the landscape.

Among the Roman towns of the region Bath stands alone, differing from the others both as a spa and because of the extent and quality of its surviving remains. Bath was among the most important spas in the Roman empire, and visitors came to bathe in the waters and to worship at the shrine of Sul Minerva from all over Britain and from the continent. The Roman walls enclosed an area of about 22½ acres, and within were the magnificent baths, the largest of their kind in Europe, and the temple building. The temple has been almost totally destroyed, but much of the baths survive and are among the most impressive Roman remains in Britain.

A unique and altogether remarkable feature of the Wessex landscape may possibly date from the late Roman period. This is the blatantly masculine figure of the Cerne Giant cut into the chalk hillside overlooking Cerne Abbas in Dorset. The massive figure still dominates the little town and the site of the former Benedictine monastery. On stylistic grounds he has been dated to the Roman period, and it has been suggested that he is intended to represent the Roman god Hercules. If he is indeed Roman or Romano-British in origin, it seems almost incredible that such a starkly pagan figure should have been allowed to survive in that position, dominating the site of an important and wealthy Benedictine monastery founded in 987. What makes the puzzle even more intriguing is that although there are several detailed surveys of the lands at Cerne, there is no mention of the Giant until the mid-eighteenth century, and no reference in local documentary sources to the scouring which would have been necessary every few years if he was to survive. The Giant remains one of the great mysteries of the Wessex landscape.

THE SAXON LANDSCAPE

The agricultural and religious developments of the Saxon period and their effect on the landscape will be discussed in the following chapters; here it is sufficient to note that after the departure of the Roman armies a long period of confused strife followed the invasions of the Saxons, and later the raids of the Vikings, and that these have left their mark on the landscape in the form of various defensive earthworks. Excavations at hill-forts such as South Cadbury and Cadbury-Congresbury as well as at Glastonbury and elsewhere are revealing new, authentic information about the dark period between the Romans and the Saxons which has hitherto been dominated by legends of King Arthur. Other earthworks and defences of this period which are still visible in the landscape include Bokerly Dyke on the Wiltshire/Dorset border, an enormous earthwork stretching for six miles across the downland and guarding the approach into Dorset from the north. It evidently presented a formidable though ultimately unsuccessful barrier against the Saxons, and still forms the county boundary. A second line of defence for Dorset was Combs Ditch, 15 miles inside

11 St Aldhelm's Chapel on the Dorset coast at Worth Matravers (National Monuments Record)

the county. Most impressive of all is the Wansdyke. Although long thought of as a single work, this is in reality two linear earthworks, West Wansdyke which runs from Maes Knoll south of Bristol to Bath, and the larger and much more prominent East Wansdyke running for some 12 miles across the Wiltshire Downs north of the Pewsey Vale. Both were probably constructed during the late fifth or the sixth centuries as a defence against Saxon attacks from the north, although the curiously indefensible route followed by the West Wansdyke, below the slope of the hills, is another of the landscape mysteries of Wessex. The East Wansdyke, however, suffers from no such defensive inadequacies and remains one of the most spectacular prehistoric earthworks of the region.

The attempt to create defences against the Viking attacks upon Wessex in the ninth century produced the 'burhs' or series of fortified strongholds planned by King Alfred from his base on the isle of Athelney in the Somerset marshlands. The finest surviving earthworks are around Wareham, where extensive remains of the great defensive banks survive. Dorchester, Shaftesbury and Bridport were similarly defended and other burhs included Watchet, Lyng, Axbridge, Bath, Cricklade—where a square defensive enclosure surrounds the town—Malmesbury, and Wilton.

It is appropriate to end this brief account of the early impact of human activity upon the Wessex landscape with the picture of the region which we can, with some difficulty, recognise in the Domesday Survey of 1086. This sums up the effects of the preceding centuries of human toil and conflict. By the time of the Survey, the pattern of settlement, the lay-out of manors and the siting of villages was already established over most of Wessex. Many of the modern village and town names are found for the first time in the Survey, much of the most fertile land was already under cultivation, and the main features of farming which were to persist throughout the Middle Ages can also be discerned. It must, however, be remembered that the Survey was not intended as a description, but was concerned with taxable units, and its detailed interpretation is fraught with difficulties.

Settlement was spread fairly evenly across the region, except for a few 'empty' or sparsely populated areas; these included much of Exmoor and the neighbouring hilly country, the marshy lands in the Somerset levels, and the barren uplands of Mendip; the large expanses of the chalk downlands in Wiltshire and Dorset were devoid of settlement outside the river valleys, since here was the only water supply; and relatively few people were to be found in the heathlands of east Dorset. As might be expected these barren, thinly-populated areas also had the least arable land as judged by the number of plough-teams listed.

The larger towns included Bath and Shaftesbury, each with about 1,000 inhabitants, and below them in size came Bridport, Dorchester, Ilchester, Malmesbury and Wareham; smaller still were such towns as Frome, Bradford-on-Avon, Milborne Port and Great Bedwyn. The most characteristic feature over much of the region was the woodland. The heavier soils in particular remained heavily wooded in spite of the Anglo-Saxon inroads which are recorded in such numerous place-name endings as 'ley' or 'leigh', meaning a woodland clearing, or in the number of place-names which incorporate a reference to some species of tree—oak, ash, beech or thorn. The Survey records heavy woodland cover in north and west Wiltshire, in the Blackmoor Vale and the western vales of Dorset and in the eastern part of Somerset. The chalk and heathlands were, however, comparatively bare of woodland. In the chalklands settlements were clustered in the valleys of the fast-flowing streams, and along these streams most of the best meadow-land of the region was to be found. Meadow is also mentioned around many Somerset villages, particularly along the rivers Brue, Cary, Parrett and Chew. Finally a degree of specialisation in land-use is recorded in the 13 vineyards which are listed, two in Dorset, seven in Somerset and four in Wiltshire. Even the usually dry, formal words of the Domesday Survey manage to show one of these places as pleasingly fertile and prosperous: the description of Wilcot in the vale of Pewsey contains the words *ecclesia nova, domus optima et vinea bona* (a new church, an excellent house and a good vineyard.)

Fields and Farms in the Wessex Landscape

Fields are by far the commonest and most universal feature of the land-scape, and like other human artefacts they have been subject to constant change and development over the centuries. It is not difficult to recognise the typical fields of various periods, and it adds greatly to the appreciation of any landscape to be able to discern such clear evidences of historical development within it. Each region in Wessex has its own distinctive fields: the small, irregular enclosures laboriously hacked out of the ancient wood-land of the clay vales; the straight-sided fields created by the drainage-channels or 'rhynes' of the Somerset levels; the regular, geometrical fields of Parliamentary enclosure, the dry-stone walls of the Cotswold fringe, and many other types. All these fields with their various kinds of hedges and fences represent the response of different generations to the problems of farming their own land most conveniently; the construction of these fields and hedges has also involved long hours of laborious toil over suc-ceeding centuries, in both their creation and maintenance. Each type of farming also has its own distinctive buildings, and the shape, size, siting and names of farm houses and farmsteads can tell us much about the agri-cultural development of each area.

'CELTIC' FIELDS

The earliest recognisable fields in Wessex are the so-called 'Celtic' fields which were described in the previous chapter. These are the small square or rectangular fields ranging from a half to two acres in extent and bounded by low banks, and their remains can be seen all over the hillsides on the chalk downlands, in places which have not been ploughed by later farmers. Good examples can be seen on Fyfield Down in Wiltshire, on Shillingstone Down or above Sydling St Nicholas in Dorset, on Bathampton Down just outside Bath and in many other places. The best time to see them is in evening sunlight when the low banks of the former hedges show up especially clearly. Those which survive must be only a small proportion of the fields which originally existed; many have disappeared during the massive attacks by the plough on the downlands during the twentieth cen-

12 Celtic fields on the Dorset downland (Photograph: J. E. Hancock)
13 Celtic fields on Bathampton Down with Bath University in the background
(Photograph J. E. Hancock)

tury. Moreover, these surviving fields are on the most marginal of land which has been shunned by later arable farmers; we can only speculate as to how much of the more fertile and easily worked land on the lower slopes of the downland were once also covered by similar fields. These fields remained in use for a long period. Excavation of the banks and of the 'lynchets' or terraces which have formed where the fields are on sloping hillsides has shown that some of these 'Celtic' fields date from the Bronze Age, others were created during the Iron Age, while more were formed during the expansion of arable farming which occurred after the arrival of the Roman armies. At a few places in the chalklands can be seen not just the fields with their low boundaries, but a whole complex of them joined by lanes and tracks and including what was obviously the farmstead. One example is at Shearplace Down near Sydling St Nicholas on the high downland of Dorset; the site consists of a small, circular, ditched enclosure which contained the farmhouse, a yard with a circular barn or farm building, and a trackway leading off through a complex of small fields, each of an acre or less bounded by the typical small banks or lynchets. This has been dated to about 1200 B.C. Another similar farm with its fields has survived at Turnworth and has been shown to date from the Iron Age. These fields were apparently arable, and the great surrounding expanses of downland were no doubt used for stock grazing. At Thorny Down, however, a series of at least nine buildings is enclosed within a rectangular earthwork of half-an-acre in extent, and this has been suggested as a stock enclosure and as a centre of pastoral farming.

In a few places on the chalk downs of Wiltshire and Dorset, where large and continuous areas of 'Celtic' fields survive, close examination has revealed a pattern of long boundaries enclosing much larger units of several hundred acres. The extent and number of these 'Celtic' fields which survive, together with the evidence of the larger, enclosing boundaries, suggests both that these areas of prehistoric England were farmed much more intensively than has hitherto been supposed, and that farming was much more highly organised and arranged in large units on a greater scale than might have been thought possible.

ROMAN FIELDS AND FARMING

Many of the 'Celtic' fields survived throughout the Roman occupation, and Iron Age farming methods no doubt continued to be used by many of the native population. But the Romans introduced an important new development in agricultural technology. This was a mould-board plough, much heavier and stronger than the primitive 'ard', and possessing the three basic essentials which all ploughs have retained ever since. The Roman plough consisted of a heavy wooden beam to which was attached an iron *coulter* for cutting the turf or sod vertically, an iron *share* which cut horizontally underneath the slice, and a wooden *mould-board* which

14 The pattern of fields on the edge of Exmoor (Photograph: J. E. Hancock)

turned the furrow over. This was an enormous advantage, and all subsequent developments of the plough have merely modified this basic idea.
The Roman plough could cultivate more deeply and provide the basis for
a better seed-bed; it could be used on much heavier land, and was an important factor in increasing the production of corn in Roman Britain. The
use of the mould-board also avoided the need for cross-ploughing, so that
no longer were square fields the most convenient shape; although the older
fields continued in use, a longer, narrower field was introduced. Examples
of such long fields, adapted to the improved plough, can be seen at Martin
Down on Cranborne Chase and at Fyfield Down near Marlborough; the
fields are about 500 ft long and 100 ft wide, bounded on all four sides with
low banks like the earlier fields. Romano-British rural settlements included
both villas and native farms, the latter continuing in many places the traditions and practices of the Iron Age. They ranged in size from single farmsteads or small groups like that at Rotherley or Woodcutts to settlements
like Chisenbury, where over 80 buildings have been identified. For both
the romanised villas and the traditional farms, arable farming for corn,
especially wheat and barley, and the raising of sheep and cattle continued
to be the basis of their livelihood, though no doubt much of the impetus
for advances in farming techniques came from the villas and from the
romanised owners of the villa estates, profiting from the increasing
demand for food both for the Roman army and for export.

One of the great unsolved problems of English landscape history is how the system of farming which has just been described developed during the period of the Saxon invasions—the Dark Ages—into the medieval pattern of common fields, farmed in strips, which was such a widespread feature of medieval farming on the lighter lands of Wessex. In the absence of any detailed documentary evidence on the subject it is impossible to be sure just how such a complex system of communal farming could have originated, not just in Wessex but also throughout the whole of midland England. The common-field system of farming has, however, had a profound effect upon the landscape, and it is this aspect of it which concerns us here. Although the system of communal or common-field farming was often highly complex in practice and varied in its details from place to place, its basic essentials were very simple. The arable land of each community consisted of two, three or more large unfenced fields, and each field was divided into strips, known variously in Wessex as 'lands', 'lawns' or 'halfs', and farmers had their strips scattered about the field. Groups or blocks of strips all aligned in the same direction were known as furlongs and each field consisted of several furlongs. The essential feature of the system was that when the strips were not under cultivation either because the crops had been harvested or because the field was fallow, then the sheep and cattle of the community were allowed to graze over the whole area, in other words the field was open for 'common' grazing.

There was no standard form or type of medieval common field, the customs of each community varied widely, and the ways in which they organised their communal farming and controlled the balance between meadow and pasture, arable and stock were also very different, just as the fields themselves and the individual strips and furlongs within them varied greatly in size. How such a complex system developed is a great puzzle, since its working required a considerable degree of communal organisation. It demanded that everyone should grow similar crops in each field which would be ready for harvesting at roughly the same time, that everyone fallowed their land in the same rotation, and that all the variations which over the centuries were made in the system by each community, were introduced by the common agreement of all through the manorial courts. Common agreement had also to be made for the way in which the livestock were managed and for the division and allocation of meadow-land which provided the essential hay crop to support the animals during the winter. In a few places in Wessex such as Keynsham and Cricklade the practice of dividing the meadow-land annually in 'doles' or 'lots' continued into the nineteenth century; and there is evidence from Congresbury, Wick St Lawrence and Puxton of the way in which the 'Dolemoors' were annually divided by drawing specially marked apples from a bag. For farmers on the light, chalkland soils of much of Wessex, however, the system, in spite of the way in which it restricted individual enterprise, had one supreme advantage which alone ensured that it survived in many places until the enclosures of the eighteenth and nineteenth centuries. The advantage consisted of the communal sheep flock. Satisfactory crops of corn could only be grown on these thin soils by the intensive use of the sheep fold, and for a satisfactory fold it was necessary to have very large numbers of sheep, folded at the rate of a thousand sheep to an acre. Few farmers could keep such large numbers and therefore all the sheep of each community were normally kept in common flocks under a common shepherd or shepherds. Each day the sheep grazed on the chalk downlands, and each evening they were brought down to be close-folded on the arable land within wattle hurdles. The fold was moved each day in a regular sequence across the arable fields. The fact that each man's strips were scattered therefore meant that all received equal benefit from the dung of the communal flock and that all had a fair share. The system of common-field farming was not, however, confined to the chalklands, though it generally survived longest there, but it was also to be found during the Middle Ages and later in many parts of the heavier lands of north Wiltshire, Somerset and north and west Dorset. The communal farming of the common-fields was not static, but could be changed and adapted to accommodate such things as an increased population, changes in farming, new crops or particular local conditions. As late as the seventeenth century new common-fields were still being made in some places. At Moreton in 1620 it was agreed to make a third arable field out of part of the downland; the new field was divided into strips and furlongs and it was ordered by the manorial court that it should be '... converted to tyllage and that it may be Somerfeyld (i.e. fallow] every thirde yeare and be eaten and ordered at the breach of the feyldes as the other two feyldes, nowe are....' In other words it was to be subject to the same common use as the existing fields. There was a similar extension of arable land at Compton Chamberlain during the early seventeenth century. At Stratford-sub-Castle in the late seventeenth century a fourth common-field was made out of the downland and was to be 'called New Field and ... to be continued arable and sowed in course as a fourth field'. There were also differences in the ways in which the course of farming in the common-fields was regulated, notably over the matter of fallows. On the better land the normal practice was to allow the land to lie fallow every third year to recover its fertility, but on poorer soils such as the island of Portland or at Mere or some parts of Amesbury and in many other places a fallow every other year was the norm.

The common-fields have had a profound influence on the landscape of Wessex. In a few places they have survived almost intact or can be seen fossilised beneath later enclosures. Most notable of the survivals are the fields on the island of Portland; here the medieval strips survive over about 150 acres and show better than anywhere else in Wessex what medieval

15 Medieval strips and field patterns surviving beneath later hedges at Keyford near Frome (Photograph: J. E. Hancock)

strip-farming must have looked like. At Corfe Castle and Kingston in east Dorset there are large areas of surviving strips; those at Corfe Castle are recorded on a map of 1585, and, as with the fields on Portland, the mere or boundary stones survive at the end of each strip. At the other end of the region a remarkable series of fossilised strip-fields survives within the ramparts of the Iron Age hill-fort of Little Solsbury in the parish of Batheaston, near Bath. Here is a remarkable example of continuing use and

16. Surviving Common Arable Fields on the Island of Portland (J. E. Hancock).

adaptation of the landscape over the centuries, for in an area close to the Fosseway and rich in Roman remains, and where traces of Celtic fields cover the hillsides, round barrows are to be seen on the skyline and the massive defences of the Iron Age hill-fort dominate the scene. On the flat hill-top, inside the ramparts of the hill-fort, an area of some 25 acres has been laid out as a complete medieval field system with the strips and furlongs, now under grass, clearly visible, their ends marked by mere stones. Close examination of the strips reveals evidence that they have later been ploughed into narrow three to five-yard ridges, a type of cultivation which was used during the eighteenth and nineteenth centuries, and is most commonly found on grassland brought back into cultivation to meet the increased demand for corn during the Napoleonic war. When the parish Tithe Map was drawn in 1840 the strips were still arable, but soon afterwards were put down to grass and have remained as pasture ever since. Little Solsbury Hill provides a remarkable example of the way in which the evidence for so many different uses over such a long period can survive in the same landscape.

But much more common and widespread is the way in which the shape of the former strips and furlongs is reflected in the shapes of the enclosures and hedgerows which have subsequently been imposed upon them. The shape of the strips in the common-fields makes it possible to recognise them even when they lie under later enclosures, for the strips were not straight but, because of the way in which they were ploughed, they assumed over the centuries a characteristic reversed 'S' shape, a shape which can still be recognised in innumerable field boundaries throughout Wessex. The reason for this shape was strictly practical. The heavy plough, or 'sull' as it was called in the west country, needed a team of six or eight oxen or a similar complement of horses to pull it; these worked in pairs, and naturally the leading beasts were a long way ahead of the plough. In the common fields where the strips and furlongs butted closely upon one another and were cultivated by different farmers, each man's plough team would inevitably go on to his neighbour's land in turning; but by ploughing in a reversed 'S' shape the team could begin and end each furrow almost at right angles to the strip they were ploughing and could avoid, at least partially, damage to neighbouring strips. In a few places the strips were in a gentle 'C' curve for the same reason. This feature of the common-fields makes them easy to recognise even though they have been enclosed, because in many places the later hedges follow the shape of the strips or enclose individual furlongs. As will be shown later this is not always the case, since Parliamentary enclosures tended to ignore previous boundaries, but in the many places where enclosure was accomplished by piecemeal agreement between the farmers the outline of the former strips and furlongs can still be recognised. Examples are to be seen all over the chalklands, but it has to be remembered that common-field farming was not confined to the light lands. Documentary evidence shows that the system was widespread on some parts of the claylands and evidence can still be seen in the field-shapes of such widely scattered places as Thornford in north Dorset, around Hinton St Mary, Shepton Beauchamp, Stoke-sub-Hamdon, Castle Cary, Alford or Melksham, and all along the low-lying land beneath the chalk scarp from Market Lavington to Westbury, and in many other places. This is indeed one of the commonest and most readily identified landscape features.

Two other features which were often associated with the common-fields, and which are widespread through the region, must also be mentioned. The first is known as *ridge-and-furrow*. This consists of long narrow ridges across the fields divided from each other by shallow ditches or furrows, giving the surface of the field a corrugated appearance. These ridges were made by the action of the plough over the centuries throwing the earth up in the same direction and gradually building up ridges; obviously they were made intentionally and are far too pronounced to be purely accidental. The most probable explanation for them seems to be that they were made in order to drain the land; it is true that they are also to be found on lighter lands where drainage was not a problem, but it may be that such a method of ploughing had merely become traditional. There is no way of dating this ridge-and-furrow, for it could be the result of ploughing with a mould-board plough which turned the furrow in one direction at any period, and some ridge-and-furrow may be relatively modern. Nor is ridge-and-furrow always associated with the common-fields, but it will be observed that many of the ridges have the characteristic reversed 'S' shape, and in some places the blocks of ridges still show the pattern of strips and furlongs in the common-fields. This is not to say that the ridges necessarily equate precisely with the strips. The strips varied in width from place to place and while in a few places a strip may have consisted of a single ridge with the furrows marking its boundary, in most fields there were two or three or more ridges to each strip.

The other landscape feature which can be seen throughout the chalk downlands is the *strip lynchets*. There are the terraces by which cultivation was extended up the hillsides thereby enabling much more land to be ploughed. Whole series of such terraces are to be seen at many places, on the chalk downs above Maiden Newton or at Bincombe and Worth Matravers, at Mere, Combe Bisset and around the Deverills, and all across the chalklands. Again these are very difficult to date, but it is clear that the labour of constructing such terraces would not have been undertaken unless there was considerable pressure on the available arable and an increased demand for food; thus many strip lynchets probably date from the population explosion of the thirteenth century. As population-pressure eased, some reverted to grass and can still be seen in a fossilised state, but many others are still in use, ploughed now by tractor.

17 Irregularly shaped fields in the Marshwood Vale, Dorset, the result of slow clearance and 'assarting' in this former thickly wooded landscape (Photograph: J. E. Hancock)

MEDIEVAL ENCLOSURES

Some strip lynchets formed part of a common-field system, others were the result of the enterprise of individual farmers, for throughout the Middle Ages there was incessant effort to bring forest and waste and down-land into cultivation, Much of this clearance of woodland and waste, or *assarting* as it was called, was done by single farmers or by small groups who created for themselves small farms with enclosed fields. Moreover in many parts of Wessex—especially on the heavier soils and the well-wooded clays or on the marginal hilly lands of north and west Somerset—there were fewer common-fields and most farming was carried on separately or *'severally'* in fields which were not farmed communally nor subject to common rights. The fields resulting from the long process of forest clearance or from the creation of *assarts* on the waste land, can generally be easily recognised by their irregular shape, small size and substantial banks or hedges, and many thousands of such fields survive. Their irregular shape reminds us of the way in which they were laboriously hacked out of thick woodland and slowly cleared of tree stumps, stones and other obstacles to the plough. The massive hedge-banks provided shelter and kept secure the cattle, for most, though not all, of these fields were in areas of pastoral farming. Recently developed techniques of hedge-dating provide at least a rough guide to assessing the age of such enclosures. From observations made on a great many dated hedges all over the country it has been shown that the average number of different shrub species in a 30-yd section of a hedge is roughly equal to the date of the hedge in centuries. In other words hedges with a large number of shrub species are likely to be much older than those with few. Another recent development has been the recognition of certain plants as good indicators of primary woodland. These are plants which do not normally reproduce themselves outside woodland, nor do they move long distances. The most common among them are bluebells, dog's mercury and wood anemone. Obviously it would be foolish to try to press such techniques too far or to suppose that they are absolutely precise, but the existence of any of these plants in a hedge provides additional evidence for supposing that such hedges were once part of primary woodland and that the fields which they surround are therefore likely to have been hacked out of the woodland.

Another feature of these small, irregular, 'assart' fields is the fact that in periods of population growth or increased demand for food, such as the thirteenth century or the Napoleonic wars, they were extended into marginal lands, and that subsequent decline in demand for food led to their abandonment. Thus in areas such as the Dorset heathlands, the higher slopes of the Quantocks and Brendons and on Exmoor, many of these irregular fields can be seen, each carefully hedged, but which have reverted to bracken and heather.

Other fields, more regular in shape, were formed throughout the Middle Ages and later in the Somerset levels by the process of drainage and by land reclamation along the coast. These fields are generally bounded not by hedges but by drainage ditches or 'rhynes'.

Documentary evidence is not lacking for this long process of *assarting* during the Middle Ages. At Whiteparish in south-east Wiltshire, which lay within the royal forest of Melchet, the Forest Eyres or lists of fines for making *assarts* show a continuing process of encroachment upon woodland and waste, and there are constant references to small enclosures being hacked out of the Forest consisting of little fields, half to two-and-a-half acres, each enclosed by a bank and hedge. All classes of medieval society were engaged in this slow process of *assarting*, and only the extent of the land involved distinguishes the rich from the poor. For example, in 1314 Ingelram de Berenger, who was steward of the royal forest of Blackmoor in Dorset, was granted permission to 'reduce to cultivation' 184½ acres of land in Hermitage parish within the royal forest; in 1269 the Abbot of Abbotsbury held 30 acres of recently enclosed land at Hilton; while at the bottom of the social ladder, at the royal manor of Gillingham in 1302 the Court Rolls record that 'Walter atte Wodeseyned gives to the Lady Queen twelve pence for a perch and a half encroachment opposite his gate paying for rent due penny a year'. In many parts of Somerset and Dorset the numbers of farm, field and place-names ending in 'ley' or 'leigh' meaning a woodland clearance, or in 'hay' an enclosure, is in itself a reminder of their origin. Good examples are to be found throughout the Marshwood Vale in west Dorset, where much of the area consists of small scattered farmsteads, each surrounded by small, irregular fields, bounded by massive banks and with narrow winding lanes joining the isolated settlements. In the parish of Whitechurch Canonicorum the evidence in the landscape that the farms are the result of the clearance of woodland and waste by individual farmers during the twelfth and thirteenth centuries is reinforced by the evidence of the farm names, each ending in 'hay' and each incorporating an early medieval personal name, such as Bluntshay, Denhay, Sminhay, Manshay and many others. At nearby Wootton Fitzpaine farm names such as Champernhayes, Meerhay and Woodhouse tell their own story.

MODERN ENCLOSURES

The period from the seventeenth to the nineteenth centuries witnessed a massive extension of enclosed fields throughout the whole region as remaining acres of waste, marshland and forest succumbed to the onslaughts of farmers, and as lands which had formerly been grazed by communal flocks and herds, including much of the downlands, were divided, apportioned and enclosed by their individual owners, and as the common arable fields were enclosed. This gradual extension of enclosure took place at first by piecemeal private agreements, and later by wholesale enclosure under Acts of Parliament. The process took long to complete, and remains of waste and common are still to be found in many places; the common arable fields survived in Wiltshire until Charlton near Donhead St Mary was enclosed in 1867 and in Dorset until Grimston fields were enclosed in 1907, while, as shown earlier, some of the land on the island of Portland continues to be farmed in strips.

There is abundant documentary evidence from the sixteenth century onwards of this process of enclosures. Some of it comes from unexpected sources. For example, during the seventeenth century the churchwardens from several parishes in the region reported that they were unable to go on their traditional journey around the parish boundaries 'beating the bounds' because of the number of hedges which now blocked the way, and that in any case such perambulations were unnecessary because the new hedges now marked the parish boundaries. Typical of many others were the churchwardens of Netherbury (Dorset) who reported in 1613

were presente (i.e. report) that by reason of ye new inclosures and multitude of hedges wee have bene for many years constrained to forbeare goinge on procession or perambulation.

Similar evidence comes from the Quarter Sessions records. For example the Dorset justices in 1630 received complaints that the roads in various parts of the county were in decay and dangerous '. . . by reason of certaine Inclosures lately made by various persons by which they have streightened (i.e. narrowed) the way'. Manorial surveys record the same process. At Ryme Intrinseca (Dorset) a survey of 1612 records that

There was a common or spacious waste ground called Woodleaze which was

18 A flock of Dorset Horn sheep being driven down to be folded on the arable fields after a day spent feeding on the ramparts of Maiden Castle. This photograph was taken in 1935 (Photograph: Museum of English Rural Life, Reading)

taken in [i.e. enclosed] about 30 years since by the Tennants ... And divided the same between them according to the proportion of everie particular tennant. And is farre more profitable than before.

The lands allotted by this enclosure were divided by hedges into regular four- and five-acre rectangular fields, which remain a distinctive feature of the landscape, contrasting very clearly both in shape and size with the earlier enclosures elsewhere in the parish.

Not all of these enclosures were accomplished without dispute. The most notable and widespread protests occurred over the disafforestation and enclosure of the royal forests during the seventeenth century. Large areas of royal forest survived around Gillingham in north Dorset, in west

Wiltshire around Melksham and Chippenham, in the forest of Melchet in south-east Wiltshire and the forests of Selwood and Neroche in Somerset. By the middle of the seventeenth century most of these forests had been cleared and enclosed into distinctive large, regular fields which are in marked contrast to the small medieval *assart* fields in the same areas. The protests arose from those who had formerly possessed rights of grazing sheep and cattle in the royal forests, and who felt that the land which they were allocated in return for the loss of those rights was insufficient or inconveniently situated. The riots in Wiltshire and Dorset during the 1620s, together with similar protests in parts of Gloucestershire provoked by the forest enclosures, constituted the largest single popular uprising in the country during the years before the Civil War. The Wiltshire antiquarian of the seventeenth century, John Aubrey, commented upon the distress caused to those with rights of common in the forest of Pewsham around Chippenham when the land was disafforested and enclosed in 1630. He quotes in verse current in his day, c 1670

When Chip'nam stood in Pewsam's wood,
Before it was destroyed,
A cow might have gone for a groat a year,
But now it is denyed.

Aubrey was obliged to admit 'The metre is lamentable'; but added '. . . the cry of the poor was more lamentable'.

A curious seventeenth-century example of enthusiasm for enclosure comes from West Parley and West Moors in the area of barren acid heathland around Poole harbour and can still be seen in the modern landscape. In 1619 the tenants of the heathland there agreed to enclosure of the lands, claiming with superabundant and totally misplaced optimism that 'a great part of the wastes with good husbandry may be improved and made good arable and good pasture'. The enclosure duly took place, but the remarkable feature of it is that, in spite of the arguments of the tenants, the value of the land lay almost entirely in its use for cutting peat and turf, and since all parts were not equally productive of peat and in order to ensure that each tenant had a fair share of good and bad peat land, the enclosures were made in very long narrow strips right across the heath. Thus for example the allotment awarded to John Bolton, one of the tenants, consisted of 15 acres in a single strip 22 yds wide and nearly two miles long. These strips were duly enclosed with banks, and the Tithe Map of 1839 shows the strips going right across the heathland, each almost two miles in length. The low banks made to divide the strips can still be seen today stretching apparently endlessly across the poor, acid soils of West Parley Heath. It is very unlikely that these strips were ever worth enclosure, and some of them have names such as 'Folly' and 'Troublefields' which tell their own story; but they remain in the twentieth-century landscape as a monument to the unwarranted optimism of their seventeenth-century owners.

During the seventeenth century further drainage work was being carried out and enclosures made in the Somerset levels, especially in the area around Long Sutton, along the coast and in the tidal estuaries of the Yeo, Axe and Parrett rivers, although the really large-scale drainage projects did not come until the eighteenth and nineteenth centuries.

The seventeenth and eighteenth centuries also saw great advances in agriculture, new crops, new fertilisers, new methods, and some of these changes have left their mark on the landscape. The pits from which marl was dug for fertiliser survive in many places, the ruins of lime-kilns are frequently to be found, and above all many thousands of acres of water-meadows which originated during the seventeenth and eighteenth centuries are still recognisable all over the region and especially in the chalk-land valleys, although very few are any longer in use. The water-meadows varied in their form in different parts of the region. In the chalklands they were constructed along the valley bottoms, whereas in parts of Somerset streams were led in leats along higher ground and made to overflow down the hillside; but the object was the same, to cover the grass during the winter with a thin sheet of moving water, thereby protecting it from frost and cold, and encouraging a much earlier and lusher growth of grass than would have occurred naturally. The 'floated' meadows of the chalklands consisted of an elaborate system of weirs, hatches, channels and drains to ensure that the water was kept moving over the surface of the meadows. These can still be easily recognised, and in other parts of the region the 'catchwork' or hillside meadows can also be discerned from the evidence of the leats and hatches which survive. The water-meadows became an invaluable system for producing early grass and large crops of hay, and throughout the chalklands they were the sheet-anchor of farming since they enabled so many more sheep to be kept through the winter, thus providing dung for a much greater acreage of corn than could otherwise be

19 The rectangular enclosures and straight lines of willow-
fringed drainage channels in the Somerset levels (Photograph:
J. H. Bettey)

20 Water Meadow at Nunton near Salisbury (Photograph: Museum of English Rural Life, Reading)

grown. Thomas Davis, the steward of the Longleat estates, summed up their value in 1794 when he wrote

... none but they who have seen this kind of husbandry, can form a just idea of the value of the fold of a flock of ewes and lambs, coming immediately with bellies full of young quick grass from a good water-meadow, and particularly how much it will increase the quantity and quality of a crop of barley.

The water-meadows of Wessex are one of the most important of all the features of former farming practice in the region.

Most of the old water-meadows went out of use during the late nineteenth and early twentieth centuries, as moden strains of grasses and modern artificial fertilisers made it possible to produce an early growth of grass. A disadvantage of the old system of water-meadows was that because of the delicate network of channels and drains they could not bear the weight of tractors or of modern haymaking machinery. The price of modern fertilisers has however created a new interest in water-meadows as a cheap means of producing early grass, and a remarkable experiment by the Ministry of Agriculture in the development of a new kind of water-meadow can be seen in the Ebble valley at Odstock, south of Salisbury. The new system depends not on channels and drains but on having the flat surface of the meadow carefully 'graded' or sloped so that the water enters at the top and gently flows across the surface of the meadow. It is hoped that this experimental idea will allow machinery to be used on the meadow, and that it may herald a revival of the Wessex water-meadows.

ENCLOSURE BY ACT OF PARLIAMENT
In many parts of Wessex the long process of gradual, piecemeal enclosure

was finally completed by Parliamentary authority. This finally brought an end to common arable fields and common grazing land, and gave to large areas an entirely new appearance. In place of the arable land in strip fields, the open chalk downland grazing and the large areas of open common lands elsewhere, was substituted a formal landscape carefully planned by professional surveyors, of rectangular fields with straight hedgerows (often composed of a single shrub species, such as hawthorn), and new straight roads with wide verges. This countryside of straight lines and right angles, cutting across all previous roads, fields and hedges, contrasted strongly with earlier landscapes and is easily recognisable. The creation of new, compact farms by Parliamentary enclosure was followed in many places by the building of new farmhouses and farm-buildings in the middle of the newly-enclosed fields and away from the villages. Such farms, generally dating from the early nineteenth century, the period of high agricultural profits during the Napoleonic Wars, are often distinguished by their names: for example in Wiltshire farms occur called Waterloo, Hougomont, New Leaze, New Grounds, Quebec and New Zealand, while in Dorset farm names such as Botany Bay, Normandy, Canada, Newfield, Quatre Bras and California reveal the date of their construction.

Great areas of chalk downland still remain unenclosed at the end of the eighteenth century. John Claridge in his *Survey of Dorset Agriculture* of 1793 wrote lyrically that 'The most striking feature of the County is the open and uninclosed parts, covered by numerous flocks of sheep, scattered over the Downs. . . .' Within the next few years these 'open and uninclosed parts' were mostly divided and separated by hedges. Some were enclosed by Act of Parliament, others by agreement among the tenants, as for example at Cerne Abbas where the extent of the former arable fields and downland grazing can still be seen from the superb viewpoint by the Giant. In some parts of the region, and especially in Dorset, the common farm-name 'Dairy House' is a reminder that in periods of high corn prices it was a regular practice for arable farmers to devote themselves to corn growing and to let their milking cows to a dairyman for an annual rent. Under this system the farmer provided the cows and the necessary pasture and winter fodder in return for an annual rent for each cow. The dairyman had to milk the cows and made his profit from the sale of milk, butter and cheese. A description of such a rented dairy occurs in Thomas Hardy's *Tess of the d'Urbervilles*. The house and buildings provided for the dairyman were commonly known as the Dairy House, and many of these have in the process of time become farms in their own right.

The process of Parliamentary enclosure, while it undoubtedly resulted in a higher standard of farming, nonetheless, often had disastrous effects for the small farmers who either could not afford the high cost of making the hedges and enclosures, or whose allotment of land in place of their former rights of grazing sheep and cattle on the commons were insufficient

21 Model Farm of 1859–60 at Eastwood Manor Farm, East Harptree
(Photograph: J. H. Bettey)

to support them and their families. Such men were compelled to sell their allotments of land to the larger farmers and join the growing class of landless labourers. Parliamentary enclosure therefore had the effect of increasing the size of farms and decreasing the number of farmers. Examples of the new, geometrically planned landscapes laid out by the surveyors appointed under the Enclosure Acts can be seen all over the region.

In Somerset much of the modern landscape of the higher land on Mendip was created by early nineteenth-century enclosure, with large regular fields, straight roads and every indication of a careful plan by a surveyor. Between 1771 and 1813 some 27,500 acres of land was enclosed on Mendip. Many of the new fields were enclosed by dry stone walls which gives the Mendip plateau its characteristic modern appearance; other fields were hedged with thorn. After enclosure and allotment of the fields to individual owners new farms were built on Mendip, many of which can still be easily recognised both by their architectural style and by their names such as Canada, Wellington, New House, Victoria, or Tynings (the Somerset word for enclosure). Such farms often consist of a farmhouse built of the local limestone, flanked on each side or enclosed around a yard by a barn, wagon-house and cattle-stalls. Enclosure with its new rectangular fields and new farms completely transformed the previously barren windswept wasteland appearance of the high Mendip plateau, and this original appearance can now only be recaptured by visiting the few remaining 'unimproved' areas such as the upper slopes of Black Down above Burrington with its spectacular views across the lowlands to Clevedon and the Severn estuary. In the Somerset Levels much drainage work and enclosure was also carried out by Act of Parliament—particularly the vast expanse of King's Sedgemoor (1796–8), but also many smaller enclosures such as the well-documented examples of Mark, Huntspill and Wedmore in 1784. In Brent Marsh to the north of the Polden Hills nearly 20,000 acres were enclosed and drained between 1780 and 1800. The enclosure and drainage of King's Sedgemoor also greatly increased the amount of agricultural land available in the Bridgwater Levels south of the Polden Hills. The effect of these and many other drainage and enclosure projects can still be clearly seen in the landscape. Modern drainage-channels have created a very distinctive landscape in this flat, lush region of pollarded willows and Friesian cows, where the fields are intersected by a multitude of small open drains or 'rhynes' full of water, which eventually flow into the great artificial channels made for the Axe, Brue and Huntspill rivers.

22 Hintonfield Farm near Hinton Charterhouse (Photograph: Neil Gibson)

In Dorset much land on the heath and on the high chalk downs underwent large-scale enclosure during the late eighteenth and early nineteenth centuries. In the clayland, Leigh Common near Sherborne was enclosed by Act of 1803, divided into rectangular fields with hedges composed of an average of one or two shrub species, and crossed by straight roads with the wide verges so characteristic of Parliamentary enclosure. A third of the parish of Holwell in the Blackmore Vale was enclosed by an Act in 1797 and the effects are still very apparent in the landscape there, including several farms new-built after the enclosure. In several parts of Wiltshire the process of enclosure can be seen from documentary evidence. Maps and surveys survive for several places showing the landscape just before enclosure and the proposals of the Parliamentary surveyors of which the results can still be seen in the landscape. At Urchfont near Devizes, for example, the total transformation of the landscape can be seen by comparing the map of 1784 which shows the common-field system in operation with the map accompanying the Parliamentary Enclosure Act of 1793 which swept away the old strip fields and created the modern landscape. The same process can be seen in even more detail at Milton Lilborne near Pewsey, where pre- and post-enclosure maps survive together with the surveyor's rough plans and notes showing the way in which the reconstruction of the landscape was planned and accomplished.

The process of enclosure went on through the nineteenth century, especially on the downlands where new fields were created as the land was brought into cultivation by mechanised ploughing, first by steam-power and later by tractors. In Somerset a spectacular example of land reclamation in the nineteenth century was on Exmoor. The enclosure of an area of some 22,000 acres of Exmoor Forest was authorised by an Act of 1815. In 1818 this large tract of undeveloped moorland was bought from the Crown by John Knight, an ironmaster from Shropshire. It was the work of the Knight family during the nineteenth century which turned much of this waste land into farms, and created the modern landscape of Exmoor.

Some areas of the region escaped enclosure altogether; generally the poorest, badly drained land or the higher moorlands. Thus large parts of Exmoor and of the Dorset heath remain unenclosed, and there are many tracts of unfenced common land in the claylands of north Wiltshire and in the northern part of Avon below the scarp of the Cotswolds.

In recent years the process of enclosure has been reversed, with the removal of many hedges in the interests of ever more complex mechanisation in agriculture. But still it is possible to discern from field shapes, hedges, field and farm names and from the remains of earlier fields which survive in many places, the complex story of the farmers' unceasing battle with the wilderness and the way in which the landscape has been changed and adapted to meet different farming needs and methods.

Villages

Many of the villages of Wessex have an air of permanence and changeless-
ness which obscures the fact that settlements are as subject to fluctuation,
expansion, contraction, alteration of shape—and even to complete desertion or destruction—as are all other man-made features of the landscape.
One immediate difficulty in discussing this subject is to differentiate
between villages and small towns. This is especially a problem in the west
country where some villages started life as planned towns, but failed to
achieve the success their founders had hoped for, while other villages in
the area are composed of such a dispersed scatter of hamlets and farms
as scarcely to be recognisable as villages at all. Villages which were originally planned as towns or which possessed markets will be discussed in the
next chapter, and for the purposes of the present chapter the rough definition will be adopted that a village is and was any rural settlement of more
than a few houses and with a parish church, but which looked to some
larger local centre for many of its needs such as markets, aspects of local
government, specialised crafts or professional services. A hamlet may be
roughly defined as a smaller, subsidiary settlement without a parish
church. Inevitably there are settlements which do not fit happily into these
definitions, and perhaps we have finally to abandon precise definition and
rely on the subjective guide of whether the inhabitants of a particular
place think of it as a town or as a village.

Even to the casual visitor the contrast is apparent between the nucleated,
compact villages of the chalklands where the houses nestle close to each
other beside a chalk stream, with few farms and cottages outside the village,
and where the church, inn, shop and school are a central focus; and the
totally different appearance of the dispersed villages, scattered farms and
hamlets of much of west Somerset, the former forest areas of east Somerset,
or the clay vales of north and west Dorset. Increasingly also hundreds of
deserted villages and settlements scattered throughout the region are being
recognised from aerial photography or from field surveys. In other places
former villages have declined to a few houses or to a single farm, although
often the parish church remains as evidence of the existence of the former

community. These remind us that villages are not permanent features of the landscape, and that they survive only as long as they fulfil a useful purpose for those who live in them; they are also a reminder that villages do not exist in isolation, but are dependent upon the continuing suitability of the site, upon a regular water supply and upon the available farming land, woodland, communications and natural resources of the area.

The recent discovery of so many more deserted medieval villages, hamlets and other settlements, and the evidence that many others have declined, moved or changed their form, has made us see the landscape in a new light. The expansion and contraction, rise and decline of rural communities has become a vital factor in our understanding of landscape history. Nonetheless most villages which do survive are very ancient, and were already established by the time of the Domesday Survey of 1086, and are there mentioned by name; many are also named and the boundaries of their territory described in detail in charters of the ninth and tenth centuries, while place-name and archaeological evidence show that others originated even earlier and were in existence in the fifth and sixth centuries. For example, the boundaries of the parish of Plush in Dorset are given in a Charter of 891, and the many other surviving early charters such as that for Wanborough and Little Hinton and Marksbury make it reasonable to assume that there were already settlements within the areas described. There was certainly a village church at Doulting in 709, for St Aldhelm, the first Bishop of Sherborne, was conducting a visitation there at the time of his death, and the saint's body was taken into the church. The existence of many Saxon 'minister' churches all over the region presupposes that communities needing their ministrations were already in existence; and the many village churches with substantial Saxon remains such as those at Bitton, Limpley Stoke, Alton Barnes, Inglesham, Melbury Bubb and Winterbourne Steepleton must indicate the existence of pre-Conquest communities at these places wealthy enough to build and maintain the churches. The Domesday Survey confirms that many settlements were already well-established in 1086, like Piddletrenthide which was already divided into the 30 hides or taxation units which give the place its name.

VILLAGES WITH A CENTRAL FOCUS

The traditional picture of the typical English village grouped around a village green is a type which is seldom found in Wessex, although a few villages with greens or central open spaces can be found such as Frenchay, Biddestone, Priddy, Lullington and High Ham. A few villages are grouped around some other central nucleus. For example Nunney is clustered around the late medieval castle; Muchelney and Cannington, Lacock, Frampton and a number of others are grouped around the sites of former religious houses, although some of these, like Lacock, have also had industrial and marketing functions and have developed away from their original

23 Nunney Castle and village (Photograph: J. E. Hancock)

focus. Others are obviously grouped around or near a great house such
as Wimborne St Giles, Badminton and Hinton St George, although such
villages have often been subject to rebuilding and replanning to provide
a picturesque approach to the great house, and as such will be considered
later. The most interesting of all examples of a village grouped around
some central feature is Ashmore on Cranborne Chase in Dorset. Here on
the high chalk downland more than 700 ft above sea level the absence of
water means that there are very few settlements. Ashmore is the exception
because it is situated around a circular pond which provided its water
supply. The village dates from the Romano-British period and has probably had a continuous existence for at least 1,600 years.

There are also a few villages or hamlets which came into existence as
the result of the clearance of forest or waste, and where a central area of
common pasture appears to have been left. Examples of this may be seen
at Hermitage, Hilfield and Glanvilles Wootton in Dorset, all of which
resulted from the clearance of the once heavily-wooded Blackmore Vale,
at Southwick, in the claylands of west Wiltshire, at Mells in east Somerset,
Ash Priors near Taunton, or at Hawkridge in the far west of the country.
Elsewhere greens or central spaces which once existed have disappeared
under later building or other changes, as at Hinton St George, where a
green is mentioned in 1523, but has since been swallowed up by changes
in the village plan and lay-out. Southbroom, which is now a suburb of
Devizes, grew up around a green, no doubt the remnants of an ancient
broom-covered tract of ground, a feature of which was a large pond, the
Crammer. The remains of the green and of the pool survive although much
encroached upon by modern housing development.

One of the interests in studying the villages of Wessex is to examine the variety of their shapes and plans, to speculate on the problem of why they should have developed in that particular place, and to look for evidence in the arrangement and quality of the buildings and open spaces, pattern of roads, structure and position of the church or manor house, of an earlier shape for the village or of changes in its size or plan. It will not always be possible for the visitor to answer the questions which arise from a close study of the situation, plan, buildings and other aspects of villages, for this is a subject fraught with difficulties, where it is much easier to question than it is to understand. Even a detailed study of the archaeological and documentary evidence may not reveal answers to all the problems posed, but it is certain that unless the visitor asks questions and at least tries to *understand* rather than merely to *look at* villages, then he will miss a great deal of interest. Merely posing the questions will in itself lead to the observation of features which would otherwise have been ignored. Much thought has been given in recent years to classification of villages into various types. The distinction has already been mentioned between the nucleated, compact villages of some parts of the region and the dispersed settlements characteristic of other parts. A contrast will also be observed between 'open' villages where there has been no one dominant landowner and where development has taken place without restriction and without control of the siting and standard of houses, and 'closed' villages where building has been tightly controlled by a single authority such as a resident lord of the whole manor. Such contrasts are to be seen throughout the regions and examples will be discussed later.

Another classification is by plan types. Three main sorts of plan are generally recognised as being applicable to the whole country—the linear village strung out along the sides of a stream, down a valley or along a road; the village grouped around an open space or green or some other central feature; and the third plan-type which has been given the ugly name 'agglomerated' and which consists of a jumble of roads and lands where the houses appear not to have any clear nucleus or focus and to be placed without any apparent plan or pattern, although closer examination used in conjunction with the evidence of early maps and surveys may disclose an original underlying pattern which has subsequently been obscured. It is helpful to bear these three main categories in mind when looking at the villages of Wessex, but in the rest of this chapter they will be considered under a number of different headings.

LINEAR VILLAGES

Many villages, especially in the chalklands, are strung out along a single street or on either side of a chalkland stream, which provided their water supply. Often such villages take their names from the stream, and commonly they almost join with other villages down the valley, as for example the villages along the Piddle in Dorset where Alton Pancras, Piddletrent-

The Cerne Abbas Giant: primitive art of dominating power (*J. E. Hancock*)

Medieval packhorse bridge at Bradford-on-Avon; although man-made, it seems a natural part of the landscape (*Neil Gibson*)

Golden Cap, Dorset. Note the complex pattern of fields (*J. E. Hancock*)

Lulworth Cove, a natural harbour neatly carved out by the sea (*J. E. Hancock*)

Early industrial Wessex: Tellisford in
Somerset (ABOVE) was the site of important
fulling-mills from the sixteenth century until
1838 (*Neil Gibson*); BELOW Harnham Mill,
Salisbury (*K. H. Rogers*)

hide, Piddlehinton, Waterston, Puddletown, Tolpuddle, Affpuddle and Turners Puddle are strung out down the valley and where there were once several other settlements which are now deserted. In the same way some villages are located along one principal road, such as Long Burton in Dorset, Martock and Long Load in Somerset, Chew Magna and Long Ashton in Avon. The element 'Long' in the names of many of these places is an indication of their shape. Long Sutton originally developed around a triangular village green, but then expanded by extending along the road to Langport and so acquired its 'Long' prefix.

NUCLEATED VILLAGES

Throughout the region there remain many villages that still occupy a compact area within the parish and where there is little or no pre-twentieth-century development outside this nucleus. The explanation for the shape of many of these villages is that they were formerly surrounded by their common arable fields and common meadow and pasture, so that it was not possible for settlement to spread outside the village; moreover since each farmers' arable land consisted of scattered strips in various parts of all the common fields, and since farming was essentially a communal enterprise, it was obviously more convenient if all the farms and houses were grouped together. Urchfont in Wiltshire is a good example of such a village, where although twentieth-century development has slightly obscured the original settlement pattern, a large-scale map of the village made in 1784 shows a classic nucleated plan. All the farms, houses, farmyards and barns are along the village street or the back-lane, spread out between the manor house at one end and the church at the other. Around each farmstead are a few small enclosures where cattle could be kept at night, and some common meadow land, while beyond stretch the common arable fields, each divided into furlongs and strips. Surrounding the common fields and extending up on to the high downland is the common pasture, where the communal sheep flocks grazed. This is a typical example of a common-field village, and many hundreds of similar examples are to be found. Not all are on the light lands: Thornford in the heavy clays of north Dorset was until the nineteenth century also surrounded by common arable fields, and the result can be seen in the fact that all the farms and houses are still situated in the compact, nucleated village.

Even though the common fields were enclosed early, they can still exercise a vital influence on the village plan. At Yetminster, also in north Dorset, there is documentary evidence for the existence of common arable fields around the village during the Middle Ages, but by the sixteenth century they had been enclosed. After the enclosure, however, it is clear that the newly created fields were allotted to the farmers not in compact blocks but scattered all over the parish. The result is that the farms have continued ever since to have their fields dispersed in this inconvenient fashion, in spite of several attempts to secure exchanges, and the village plan remains nucleated, with almost all the farms situated within the village. Another clayland village which is a model of the nucleated plan-type is Stour Provost near Shaftesbury. All the lands there, nearly 3,000 acres in extent, belonged to the Provost and Fellows of King's College, Cambridge. A detailed survey of 1575 shows that besides numerous small enclosures around the village there was common meadow-land along the banks of the Stour, three large common arable fields, North, South and East fields, where the tenants had all their arable, 1,300 acres of common grazing-land and eight large coppices of woodland which the College kept in its own hands and which were a profitable source of income. The common arable fields were enclosed by agreement between the College and its tenants in 1620, but the shape of the village has remained largely unaltered, with most of the houses and farms clustered around the parish church on the banks of the Stour and very little development outside the village confines.

There can be little doubt that the existence of communal farming and of common arable fields was a powerful element in the creation and survival of a great many nucleated villages, but in some places there was another practical reason for the survival of the nucleated village plan. This was the need for a water supply. All along the edge of the chalklands, and along the lower slopes of the Mendip, Quantock, Blackdown and Brendon Hills, there are strings of villages situated at the springline (the point where the springs emerge from the hillsides). The lands of such villages are often arranged in rectangular blocks running from the low-lying ground along the valley bottoms up on to the high downland or hill-top grazing and including meadows on the lower land, the common arable fields immediately below and above the village and the pasture on the highest land. Examples of such groups of villages can be seen along the lower slope of the Quantocks at Bicknoller, Halsway, Crowcombe, Bagborough and Cothelstone.

Along the spring-line at the foot of Mendip there is a line of villages between Wells and Cheddar whose lands extend from the marshlands below up on to the high bleak hilltop: these include Wookey, Westbury-sub-Mendip, Rodney Stoke and Draycott.

In Wiltshire there are also several such groups including the villages all along the lower slopes of the northern edge of Salisbury Plain, from Westbury through Bratton and Edington to West Lavington. These villages are actually situated on a belt of Greensand between the chalk and the clay vale, where an unfailing water supply is available and where they have easy access both to the meadow land in the valley and to the arable land and the downland above. Documentary evidence, together with the evidence of the regular planned layout of the lands of each village, make it clear that these settlements along the spring-line are very ancient, and that their lands are divided one from another by boundaries which date from long before the Norman Conquest.

Similar examples of such long narrow parish-shapes are to be found in Dorset, where in the chalkland valleys the parishes extend from the chalk streams up on to the high downland, and thus include all types of land. As in Wiltshire, the villages are situated in the valleys or along the spring-lines. Examples can be seen in the valleys of the Cerne, Piddle, Winter-borne, Tarrant and Gussage rivers. The obviously planned layout of such parishes is illustrated most dramatically by East Coulston in Wiltshire which, before modern boundary changes, was four and a half miles long and only half-a-mile wide, and extended from little more than 150 ft above sea level up to 700 ft on the downs.

DISPERSED SETTLEMENTS AND HAMLETS

In the heavier lands and especially in areas which were formerly heavily forested, a totally different settlement-pattern can be seen, and villages, where they exist at all, are quite different in form. Many of these settle-ments came into existence during the early Middle Ages as population expanded, new land was brought into cultivation and as more and more inroads were made upon the forest, waste and marshland. The origins of many of such settlements are apparent from their names, many of which contain elements such as 'leigh' or 'ley' meaning a forest clearing. For example, the whole area around Frome, in the ancient forest of Selwood, has a mass of such names—Orchardleigh, Berkley, Corsley, Bradley, Whatley, Leigh—indicating their origin as forest settlements. The evi-dence for the same expansion of settlement can be seen in the settlement-patterns in the Marshwood Vale in west Dorset, in the hill country of west Somerset, or in the heavy clays of north Wiltshire. In these regions there are few large villages, but a dispersed pattern of hamlets and farmsteads, created as settlement was slowly and laboriously pushed back into the less easily cultivated lands by successive generations of farmers, just as in other areas the available arable land was being extended by the creation of strip lynchets. In some of these areas it is difficult to find the village at all, for the parish church is frequently isolated or is situated in one of the hamlets and serves a large scattered community composed of farms and small groups of houses. Examples of this can be seen at Holnest, Hilfield and Hermitage and neighbouring parishes near Sherborne, or at nearby Glan-villes Wootton and North Wootton, where the second element in the name means 'Wood Settlement' and tells us its origin. The same origin for the settlement-pattern is apparent in west Dorset at Whitechurch Canoni-corum, Wootton Fitzpaine, Wootton Abbas and Marshwood, an area of remote farms and hamlets, isolated churches, and a few large settlements. At Hazelbury Bryan in north Dorset a beautifully drawn and highly de-tailed map of the parish made for the Earl of Northumberland in 1607 by a leading cartographer of the time, Ralph Treswell the younger, shows clearly the origin of the dispersed settlements there as the result of medieval

24 The village green at Biddestone (National Monuments Record)

expansion into the forest cover of this heavy clay soil. There are several single farmsteads, and three hamlets, Kingston, Wonston and Droop; the parish church is situated at Droop. This highly dispersed pattern survives today and there is still no main village, although both Kingston and Wonston are now larger than the settlement around the church at Droop. Other examples of such settlement patterns can be seen in the parishes around the edges of Exmoor, and at Penselwood, Cucklington and Stoke Trister in south-east Somerset, or at Kilmington and Horningsham over the border in Wiltshire. New settlements continued to be made from wastes and commons until recent times, and the more recently established of these can be considered under a separate heading.

SQUATTERS' SETTLEMENTS

Throughout the region there are hamlets and settlements which have come into existence during the past three or four centuries, either on the edge of existing villages or in previously open areas where there was no dominant authority and where cottages could be erected without restraint. These represent the last stage in the long process of extending settlement into previously waste land, and most of such settlements are on marshland, downs or poor commons, which had been rejected by earlier settlers. The original squatters were generally labourers who could find nowhere else to live, and many of the cottages started as no more than hovels of cob (i.e. a mixture of mud and straw) and thatch, put up overnight on some piece of common or waste ground in the commonly held, though quite mistaken, belief that such rapid construction gave the builder squatters' rights. Many of such insubstantial hovels have of course disappeared, others have been rebuilt many times and the present substantial dwellings on the site often belie their flimsy origins. An example of the way in which such labourers' cottages could be set up is seen in the Court Rolls of the manor of Cranborne, where in 1625 some of the tenants complained to the Earl of Salisbury's steward that many squatters had settled on the waste lands of the manor, thereby depriving the tenants of grazing land for their sheep and cattle. They also complained that 'Richard Cooke intends either this night or the next to set up a house (which he hath already framed) upon the common of Aldershot, and hath placed straw upon the common in the place he hath made choise of to erect his howse in ...'

Many examples of such squatters' cottages survive as single dwellings on small pieces of land by roadsides, but where waste or common land was available small communities or hamlets came into existence in this way. There are many documentary references to the growth of such settlements during the sixteenth and seventeenth centuries. For example, at Netherbury (Dorset) in 1626 a complaint was made to the Quarter Sessions that '... there are now Latelie erected eight or ten poor Cottages, on which divers poor people dwell ...' A squatters' community grew up on the waste land on the edge of Warminster Common in Wiltshire; during the seventeenth century the community consisted of only a few houses, but it grew steadily as more and more squatters arrived, until by 1781 there were more than 1,000 people living there in some 200 cottages and hovels and in appalling conditions without a proper water supply or sanitation. The place became notorious for violence, crime and drunkenness.

A whole string of such squatters' settlements is to be found on the large expanses of wastes, heaths and commons which were formerly part of the forest of Kingswood. In some places these have been overlaid or obscured by recent housing developments, but ample evidence survives for such settlements at Oldland Common, Bridgeyate, Siston Common, Webb's Heath, Coalpit Heath and the surrounding district. Perhaps the best example in Avon is to be found in the parish of Hawkesbury to the east of Wickwar. Here there are two large areas of common—Hawkesbury and Inglestone Commons—the latter showing a typical pattern of haphazardly-sited cottages, obviously established originally by squatters who set up their dwellings on this poor, ill-drained area and depended on keeping a few livestock on the large common for part of their livelihood. The manorial records of Urchfont record that during the late sixteenth century no less than 33 cottages were erected by squatters on the waste land in the manor. Most were evidently no more than hovels rapidly put up over night, for the dimensions are given and they ranged from a tiny hut 10 ft by 8 ft up to the largest which was only 16 ft square.

Occasionally such squatters' settlements can be recognised by the ironic names they were given such as Scotland, Ireland, Little London, by the element 'Common' in their place-name, or by the way in which they are obviously planted on top of older road patterns or boundaries and away from the older centres of settlement. Other ironic names for such settlements include World's End and Bineham City; the latter is a deserted village near Long Sutton which was originally called Benham: it was still occupied in 1720 although it had been in decline from at least the seventeenth and had finally ceased to be occupied by the mid-eighteenth century.

A classic example of a squatters' settlement around a piece of common land is to be seen at Broughton Common in the parish of Broughton Gifford near Melksham. Here the large circular common occupies several acres, and is surrounded by the houses of squatters. This example illustrates all the ways in which such settlements can be recognised on the ground in spite of subsequent rebuildings and alterations. It is set on a large piece of common land half-a-mile from the village, the houses are situated all around the edge of the common, are obviously of different dates and also vary greatly in plan, design and appearance, and have clearly been greatly altered, extended and modified over the years. Moreover they are totally haphazard in their position, obviously tucked in to any available piece of land.

Documentary sources confirm the landscape evidence of the way in which the settlement on Broughton Common came into existence. From the nineteenth century there was no resident lord of the manor living in the parish and there was little control over the settlement of squatters. All the arable land in the parish was enclosed by 1783, but the badly drained and unhealthy common remained open. Cottages were erected all around the common during the late eighteenth and early nineteenth centuries and created the situation which exists today. The settlement was without adequate drainage or a clean water supply, and, like many other such communities, it was at first a very unhealthy place in which to live. In 1851, for example, there was an outbreak of scarlet fever in Broughton Gifford during which 17 people died, but the mortality was confined to those living on Broughton Common. Here as in so many other places which originated as groups of squatters' hovels, subsequent rebuildings and the provision of drainage and piped water have transformed the hamlet into an attractive and interestingly situated settlement.

The modern villages and hamlets that have developed out of such 'squat-

54

25 Eighteenth-century prosperity reflected in the village
street at Freshford (Photograph: Neil Gibson)

26 Medieval bridge and eighteenth-century manor house at Iford
in the Frome Valley, near Bradford-on-Avon (Photograph:
Neil Gibson)

ters' settlements can still be recognised by their physical appearance and plan. Many are on marginal, poorly drained land or on hillsides or on small plots on roadside verges, most are remote from any ancient parish church or manor house; above all, such settlements can be recognised by their haphazard appearance, the houses all of different dates, styles and sizes, and not arranged in any regular fashion but scattered irregularly over the available land evidently at the whim of each original builder. Another common feature of such squatters' settlements is the existence of an early nonconformist chapel, as for example at Broughton Common, Dilton Marsh, Southwick and North Bradley in west Wiltshire; for although such communities were often ignored by the Church of England they proved fruitful ground for early itinerant nonconformist preachers—Baptists, Congregationalists, Quakers, and later, Methodists.

PLANNED AND ESTATE VILLAGES

In marked contrast to the unregulated, haphazard arrangement of squatters' settlements are the carefully planned and controlled estate villages, of which there are many examples in Wessex. One of the major characteristics of the region is that it has traditionally been dominated by great landowners and large estates, and estate villages are correspondingly numerous and varied. Many are of course easily recognised by their consciously 'picturesque' appearance, and were often built as much to provide a decorative entrance to the landowner's estate as for the benefit of the tenants; others came into existence as the result of benevolent attempts to provide better housing for rural labourers; while yet others were founded in furtherance of some religious or political idealism or some industrial project.

The best-known of such villages in Wessex is Milton Abbas. Between 1770 and 1790 Joseph Damer, later Earl of Dorchester, completely demolished and removed the sizeable market town with its market, shops, almshouses, grammar school and four inns, in order to make a new park around his mansion. He replaced the town by a much smaller settlement— the little village set in a deep fold of the downland a mile from his house and well out of sight. The new village consisted of 40 uniform whitewashed cottages with thatched roofs, set out on each side of a long sloping street. Most were originally semi-detached and entered through a common front door. In addition, the Earl built a row of almshouses and a new church for the village. The village of Milton Abbas remains little altered, and is certainly a most attractive planned village as well as being the supreme example in the region of imperious aristocratic powers. During the same period in east Dorset the entire village of More Crichel was moved by the landowner Humphrey Sturt, away from his mansion and park to a new site at Newtown a mile away, although here little of the new village survives.

Many examples of cottages or even of entire villages rebuilt in a consciously 'picturesque' style are to be found in the region. Perhaps the best is the Duke of Beaufort's estate village at Great Badminton with its assorted lodges, almshouses and rustic dwellings, including several *cottages ornés*. Other similarly decorative villages and hamlets are to be seen at Erlestoke, Tollard Royal and Sandy Lane in Wiltshire, Selworthy and Lympsham in Somerset, Little Bredy and Canford in Dorset. William Cobbett in *Rural Rides* described Erlestoke in 1852,

After Eddington I came to a hamlet called Earl's Stoke, the houses of which stand at a few yards from each other, on the two sides of the road; every house is white; and the front of every one is covered with some sort or other of clematis, or with rose-trees, or jasmines. It was easy to guess that the whole belonged to one owner; and that owner I found to be a Mr. Watson Taylor, whose pretty seat is close by the hamlet, and in whose park-pond I saw what I never saw before, namely some *black* swans....'

In many places groups of cottages are to be seen which were obviously built by benevolent landowners concerned to provide improved dwellings for their labourers. William Champion, a Quaker industrialist, developed a scheme of model housing for his employees during the 1790s at Warmley on the outskirts of Bristol. But the most picturesque and self-consciously romantic group of houses is to be seen at Blaise Castle near Bristol, where John Harford, a Quaker banker, built in 1810 a small hamlet of highly decorative cottages arranged around a green. Designed and laid out by John Nash and George Repton, each cottage is different, and each represents a new experiment in the contemporary search for attractive yet practical dwellings for the poor. Blaise Hamlet became very famous and the houses were much copied. Finally, at East Tytherton near Chippenham is an example of a different kind of planned village: this is a Moravian settlement founded there by John Cennick in 1745. The Moravians were a German protestant sect who during the eighteenth century founded several such villages as idealistic experiments in community living. At East Tytherton the buildings are of brick and face on to an open green; they consist of a chapel, minister's house, a large school and several attractive dwellings for the members of the community. John Cennick, who had been a friend and follower of John Wesley before joining the Moravians, is remembered as the author of the hymn 'Children of the Heavenly King'. Earlier, in 1741, he had been concerned with the building of the Kingswood Tabernacle, the first meeting house erected by the followers of the great evangelical preacher George Whitefield, who pioneered open-air preaching to the miners of Kingswood near Bristol.

INDUSTRIAL VILLAGES

The present rural and agricultural atmosphere of Wessex villages belies the fact that until the nineteenth century a great many different crafts and industries were to be found in the villages of the region, and that many were predominantly industrial. The 1801 Census showed that in many west country villages more than half of the working population was engaged in manufacturing. Weaving, spinning and other activities connected with the textile trade were most common, but there were many others—metal-working, rope- and net-making, button- and glove-making, linen, sailcloth, hats and bonnets, stays, matches, soap, candles, leather and a host of other trades were carried on in villages, for this was the industrial area of England. The noise, stench and pollution attendant upon many of these trades—especially metal working and flax and leather processing—must have made life hideous for the inhabitants.

Some villages are easily recognisable as having come into existence around one specific industry or industrial site as, for example, the villages in the cloth-producing area of south and west Wiltshire or east Somerset such as Castle Combe, Biddestone, Lacock, Beckington, Croscombe, Mells and many others; the settlements around the Radstock–Midsomer Norton coal-mining district; the hamlets in west Somerset or on and around Mendip which owed their origin to metal mining. Villages and hamlets also grew up around important canal ports or railway junctions. Several such settlements are to be found along the Kennet & Avon Canal through Wiltshire, such as Honey Street, Wilcot Green and Burbage Wharf, Dunball on the Parrett estuary near Bridgwater, or Curload on the river Tone. The expansion of James Fussell's edge-tool manufacturing industry in Somerset led to a great expansion of settlement at Whatley, Great Elm and Mells and to a new settlement at Chantry where Fussell built for his workers a church consecrated in 1846. The expansion of the glass industry led to the dramatic increase in the size of Nailsea during the nineteenth century, while settlements on Portland and in Purbeck, and around Box and Chilmark owed their origin to the quarrying industry.

DESERTED AND DECLINED VILLAGES

Recent archaeolgical work coupled with aerial photography has shown that there are many more deserted village-sites in the region than was previously supposed. Settlements have been deserted at various times and for different reasons, and no longer is it possible to attribute all desertions to the effects of the Black Death of 1348–49, severe though the impact of this plague was in the west country. Here it is possible to indicate just a few of the factors and give examples of a handful of such villages. Throughout the chalklands of Wiltshire and Dorset there are scores of examples of villages which were deserted or were greatly reduced in size during the later Middle Ages, and no doubt some of this was caused by the Black Death and by subsequent plagues during the later fourteenth century. In many cases these settlements were on marginal land, and some were the result of the extension of settlement under the pressure of population increase during the twelfth and thirteenth centuries. The fourteenth and fifteenth centuries saw a retreat from this marginal land. At Bardolfeston near Puddletown only the clearly distinguishable mounds and hollows mark the site of the houses and the former street of this sizeable village which had ceased to exist by the fifteenth century. Similarly at Gomeldon near Salisbury excavation has revealed that after a long period of occupation the small settlement was finally deserted during the later Middle Ages. There are many similar examples, and it is probably that these were abandoned because of the plagues and subsequent decline in population. But other late medieval desertions came about because of the creation of parks for deer. For example, just south of Salisbury along the Avon valley the road to Downton makes two long and apparently needless detours. Both detours take the road around medieval parks, Standlynch and Barford, and the creation of both these parks involved the destruction of a village and the eviction of the villagers. Today only Standlynch Farm and Barford Park Farm bear witness to the former existence of these settlements. At Wilton the Herberts destroyed a large part of the common-field of Washerne to enlarge the park around their house, provoking violent but useless riots there in 1549; and in north Wiltshire during the sixteenth century the Dukes of Somerset created a great new park at Savernake, leading to fruitless complaints from their tenants that they 'should have no manner of common for their beasts which would be to their utter undoing. . . .'. Other villages were destroyed to make sheep-runs during the fifteenth and sixteenth centuries.

The process of desertion can be seen at work in a group of parishes in south Dorset. These villages were in the valley of the south Winterborne, and the lands belonged to Sir William Fyllol. In 1521 his tenants at Bincombe complained that he was trying to evict them in order to keep sheep, while his tenants at nearby Winterborne Came complained that their lands were over-run by his sheep. They stated that 'because of the greate oppressions and injuries' they would not be able to pay their rent 'nor be Able to Abide in their countrey by cause of the saide greate oppressions'. It is clear that their complaints were in vain, for all along the south Winterborne valley there is a string of deserted village sites—Winterborne Herringston, Farringdon, Germayne, Came and Whitcombe. It is also clear from later evidence that the reason for all these desertions was because of eviction of the tenants in order to provide sheep pasture. During the sixteenth century all of these had been populous places, each with its parish church, but by the time of the Hearth Tax returns of 1662 very few houses remained. It was of these villages, and particularly of Winterborne Farringdon, that Thomas Gerard wrote in 1630, '. . . a lone church, for there is hardlie any house left in the Parish, such of late hath beene the Covetousness of some private Men, that to increase their Demesnes have depopulated whole parishes'.

Good examples of deserted and declining villages can also be seen very

27 Part of Blaise hamlet, designed by John Nash (Photograph: Gordon Kelsey)

well in the Wylye Valley. The site of the former village of Hill Deverill is clearly visible as a series of earthworks marking the former houses and cottages in a field just south of Longbridge Deverill, while the villages of Brixton Deverill, Monkton Deverill and Kingston Deverill, each with its parish church, are all obviously much smaller than once they were.

The process of desertion or decline continued during the eighteenth century. In some places it was caused by changes in local industry. At Holcombe new coal mines were opened a mile from the old village so that the inhabitants moved to the new site, leaving the parish church there quite isolated and now surrounded by fields and woods. At Cameley most of

the inhabitants moved during the eighteenth century to the turnpike road at Temple Cloud which was also nearer to the coal mines, and the former site now consists of the church and a couple of farms.

The enthusiasm of eighteenth-century gentry families for surrounding their mansions with carefully landscaped parks and views also led to the removal of villages. The example of Milton Abbas in Dorset has already been mentioned. Another is the small settlement of Craft or Hintonscraft in the parish of Hinton St George near Crewkerne; this is first mentioned in 1280 and the settlement continued until the mid-eighteenth century, when extensions to the Poulett's park around their great mansion at Hinton

House absorbed the last holdings and depopulated the settlement.

Desertions have not entirely ceased in the twentieth century, for in two classic cases the villagers at Imber in Wiltshire and Tyneham in Dorset were evicted by the military authorities during the Second World War, in order to create training and gunnery areas, and have never been allowed to return although public access is now permitted regularly to Tyneham and occasionally to Imber.

As well as total desertions many villages have suffered from declined populations at various periods and the careful observer should look for evidences of former house sites, lanes and streets around existing villages. In particular the nineteenth century saw a great depopulation of many villages, especially after the severe decline in agriculture during the 1870s, and notwithstanding the population increase and influx of commuters and other influences upon villages during the twentieth century, many have never recovered from the population losses of that time.

VISUAL EVIDENCE OF DEVELOPMENT OR DECLINE IN VILLAGES

By careful observation of a village, and by asking the right questions concerning the plan and layout, the quality of buildings, the character of streets, lanes and alley-ways, and by looking for the information that can be gleaned from the parish church and other public buildings, the interested visitor can learn much of the history of Wessex villages. A cursory examination will only reveal a small part of the full story, but it is an essential starting point, and adds greatly to the interest of even the most casual visit. The first question is to ask how the village relates to such features as the church, the manor house or to the road-patterns of the area? In some places such as Old Dilton, Holcombe, Cameley, Oldbury-on-the-Hill or Tarrant Crawford the village has obviously moved, leaving the church isolated. Elsewhere evidence can be found that the church is smaller than once it was, as at Upavon where the whole of the south aisle has been demolished, possibly indicating a declined population. At East Lydford the ruins of the former medieval church can still be seen on a low-lying site by the river Brue, while the present village is half-a-mile away and has a new church dedicated in 1866. Another example of a village which has moved occurs just over the Hampshire border at Sherfield English. Here, as at Cameley, it was a turnpike road that caused the development of a new village along the road and away from the old centre which gradually declined. Thus at Sherfield the parish church was rebuilt on a new site by the turnpike road during the nineteenth century, and the medieval church was allowed to fall into ruin.

The road-pattern of the area is also an important factor determining the rise or decline of villages. Throughout the region it is notable how the Saxon villages avoided the Roman roads, so that even today there are very few villages along their length. Clearly, for the Saxon settlers the great

28 Deserted Modern Village: Tyneham on the Dorset coast. The village was evacuated during the Second World War so that the area could be used as an Army firing range. The photograph shows part of the village street with the former post office and telephone kiosk; the recently restored church is almost hidden in the trees (Photograph: J. H. Bettey)

Roman roads spelt danger for they could very rapidly bring hostile forces into a settlement. Saxon villages were therefore sited two or three miles on either side of the road, a pattern which is very evident all along the Fosse Way through Avon and Somerset and all along Ackling Dyke from Salisbury to Dorchester. Later, roads brought trade and prosperity and changes of route could be disastrous, just as those villages which were missed by the railways during the nineteenth century declined rapidly in consequence. The coming of the railways to Dorset for example, brought overnight prosperity to Maiden Newton, Sturminster Newton and Gillingham, and they transformed Bournemouth within a few years from a small village to a major resort—but they also brought depression and neglect to formerly busy villages and markets which were not on a railway-line, such as Cerne Abbas, Bere Regis, Beaminster, Evershot, Shaftesbury and Cranborne.

The parish church and churchyard, the extent of restorations, the costliness of furnishings and above all the wealth or poverty revealed in tombs, monuments and headstones, will provide abundant evidence of the prosperity or depression of the village at different periods, as well as information about important village families and local crafts and industries. Good examples of this may be found in Wiltshire in the splendour and magnificence of the churches and in the costliness of the sumptuous monuments and tombstones at Steeple Ashton, Biddestone, Castle Combe, Colerne, Lacock and Bromham. All these and others in the same area provide

63

conclusive evidence of the wealth and prosperity which came from the cloth trade from the fifteenth to the nineteenth centuries. Similarly the fact that so many Dorset churches were zealously restored and often completely rebuilt during the nineteenth century is an indication of the wealth of the gentry families who paid for the work and whose elaborate monuments are now such a prominent feature of the scraped and polished church interiors. The late fifteenth- and early sixteenth-century towers of Somerset, so expensive and elaborately decorated, tell their own story of the wealth of the village communities at that period. Equally the remarkably fine nonconformist chapels in widely scattered places such as Frome, Bridport, Poole and Taunton, or the host of chapels of different denominations to be found in almost every village, say a great deal about the social as well as the religious life of the villages.

The buildings of the village should be carefully examined, with the question always in mind—what do they tell us about the history of the villages and the village community? Ideally not just the fronts of the houses, shops and other buildings should be looked at but the sides and backs also, for in many places new façades have been added to older buildings so that the present appearance of such places as Marshfield, Somerton, Marlborough, Wimborne Minster and a host of smaller places belies the true age of the buildings behind the frontages. In many chalkland villages such as Urchfont, Piddlehinton, Sydling St Nicholas and dozens of others, the existence of what are obviously former farms along the village street is a clear indication of the important part played by common-field agriculture in the life of the communities up to the nineteenth century. In some Wiltshire and Somerset villages such as Corsham, Rode, West Lavington, Beckington, Southwick and North Bradley weavers' sheds and shops can be identified. In Stoke St Gregory, Lyng and neighbouring villages in that part of the Somerset lowlands, the sheds adjoining the houses have traditionally been used for the preparation of withies. The fine seventeenth-century houses at Nunney, Batcombe, Croscombe, Yetminster, Abbotsbury and Netherbury are evidence of the prosperity which these communities enjoyed at that period, just as the elegant eighteenth-century buildings in Biddestone, Frenchay, Corsham or Puddletown are eloquent of the wealth and confidence of their builders. Equally the fine nineteenth-century shop-fronts of Mere, Beaminster, Castle Cary, Sturminster Newton or Thornbury tell us much about their importance as market centres at that period.

The public buildings in villages are also most revealing. The number, size and opulence of the inns and pubs is an obvious sign of the wealth of the community. Former markets or coaching-routes such as Hindon, Pensford, Beaminster or Marshfield may be recognised by the size and number of their inns and by the buildings around the central area which are obviously former inns. The existence of village almshouses such as

64

those at Wimborne St Giles, Long Ashton, Bishop's Lydeard, Beaminster, Corsham, Heytesbury and Froxfield, or village schools such as those at Martock, Box, Evershot, Yetminster, Mildenhall, Crudwell and Norton St Philip, will reveal the charity of prosperous local landowners or industrialists, just as estate cottages of the kind to be found at Sandy Lane, Tollard Royal, Erlestoke, Wimborne St Giles or Selworthy will reveal their concern both for the picturesque and for the well-being of the labourers on their estates.

Other buildings and sites to look for include rectories and vicarages, often fine Georgian buildings, illustrative of the rise in the wealth and status of many of the clergy during the eighteenth century: good examples may be seen at West Lavington, Chilton Foliat, Crudwell, Donhead St Mary, Puddletown, Bitton, Farrington Gurney, and Compton Pauncefoot. An example of an earlier vicarage may be seen at Bemerton near Salisbury, where the seventeenth-century parsonage house, once occupied by the saintly George Herbert who was rector there, survives.

Industrial buildings such as mills, blacksmiths', farriers', carpenters' and wheelwrights' shops can often be recognised even though they are no longer used for their original purpose. Numerous maltings can be found turned into dwellings and can be recognised by their vented conical or pyramidal roofs; fine examples of former maltings also survive in New Park Street, Devizes, in Pound Street, Warminster and in Leigh Road, Westbury. At Falfield in Avon, Chapel Allerton and Walton in Somerset and elsewhere former windmills survive as dwellings while at East Knoyle in Wiltshire a former windmill is used as a summerhouse. At Rowde a former water-mill is now a dwelling, while at Shawford a former woollen mill has been turned into a small opera house; at Street the former tannery is now a Cooperative stores. Earlier industries also leave evidence in the shape of workers' houses. Thus the brass-working industry of the Chew valley south of Bristol can be traced in houses such as Paradise Row in Woollard, built to house workers in the nearby battery mills and still bearing the date 1782. Another good series of eighteenth-century artisans' cottages can be seen at Monkton Combe. Early schools can often be recognised even though no longer used as such—good examples may be seen at Box, Norton St Philip, Yetminster, Evershot, Corsham, Cricklade and Crudwell—and schools built by one or other of the two great nineteenth-century societies can still be seen in many villages—the National Schools built for the Church of England by the National Society, and the Nonconformist schools erected by the British and Foreign School Society and often bearing the legend 'British School'.

SURVIVING EVIDENCE

In the same way former nonconformist chapels, now turned into dwellings, shops, garages or used as stores and workshops, can often be recognised. West-country villages also often have surviving lock-ups, and good examples may be seen at Box, Kingsbury Episcopi, Merriott, Bromham, Pensford, Castle Cary, Luckington, Swanage and many other villages. The lock-up at Swanage has over it the inscription

Erected for the Prevention of Vice and
Immorality by the Friends of Religion
and Good Order   A.D. 1803.

At Kilmersdon the former lock-up has been converted into a bus shelter. The village stocks also survive in many villages, often now in the church porch, and the stocks, the lock-up and the modern police station form a natural progression in the story of village law-enforcement. In the same way a progression can be seen in some villages from the parish poorhouse which survives, for example, at Chew Magna, Mere and Purton, to the grim workhouses erected after the reform of the old poor law in 1834. Good examples of the large, forbidding 'Union Workhouses' erected to serve groups or 'unions' of parishes after 1834, can be seen at Williton, Cerne Abbas, Keynsham, Flax Bourton, Semington and Clutton.

    The advantage of looking at villages in this way, searching all the time for evidence in the lay-out and buildings of the history of the place and of the successive communities who have lived there over the centuries, is that all parts are seen to have an equal role in the development of the settlement. Thus the Norman arch in the parish church and the modern council estate are both parts of the same continuing story, and the bungalows of the 1930s at one end of the village can be regarded as evidence of the same sort of expansion that created a seventeenth-century squatters' settlement around the common land at the other end. By regarding the whole fabric and layout of a village as a piece of historical evidence, and by looking for the information that the buildings and their arrangement can give concerning the rise or decline, prosperity or adversity of the community—in other words by using what survives in the village in the same way that an historian uses a document or an archaeologist examines an artefact—the visitor will get beyond a superficial view to some understanding of each village as a living, changing organism.

Towns and Market-places

Towns, markets and fairs occupied an essential role in the life of the rural communities of Wessex, providing an outlet for surplus agricultural produce, a source of all those necessities and luxuries that could not be home-produced, and a great range of legal, financial, business and administrative services. Consequently towns were numerous while markets and fairs were even more widespread, so that few places in the region were more than ten miles from some centre which, however small it might be, could nonetheless provide urban services. The former markets in many of these small towns have long since ceased to exist and there is often now little to distinguish them from the surrounding villages or to recall the important part they once played in the life of the district. In the same way many of the fairs which were once such an important and colourful part of the local scene have come to an end, leaving even less trace in the landscape of their former economic and social importance. Some of the earliest towns have already been mentioned in Chapter 1—the Roman towns such as Durno-varia (Dorchester), Lindinis (Ilchester), Bath and Cunetio (near Marl-borough); and the towns which grew out of King Alfred's creation of *burhs* or strongholds such as Wareham, Malmesbury or Cricklade. This chapter will be concerned with the later development of towns and with their place in the landscape.

TOWNS AT THE TIME OF THE NORMAN CONQUEST

The statistics in the Domesday Survey of 1086 on towns are incomplete and for many places present more puzzles than answers, but using this information in conjunction with other evidence such as that of charters or the archaeological record of the existence of mints we can construct an overall picture of the early medieval towns in the region. By far the largest and most important town was Bristol, a royal possession with a military garrison dominating the surrounding area, and already a centre of trade, paying dues to the King comparable with those paid by such important towns as York, Lincoln and Norwich. Even so the settlement at Bristol was small, a little trading community on the north side of Bristol bridge, tightly encircled by the two rivers Avon and Frome and soon to be over-shadowed on the east by the huge Norman castle. Below Bristol in size and population came the surviving Roman foundation at Bath, with a population of perhaps 1,000 in 1086; similar in size was the hill-top town of Shaftesbury, one of Alfred's *burhs* on its easily defended site where a richly endowed nunnery had also been established by Alfred with his daughter as the first abbess. Other locally important towns with markets and mints, providing a focus for economic life although they were themselves little larger than many of the surrounding villages, included the two former Roman towns of Dorchester and Ilchester and the *burhs* at Malmesbury, Bridport and Wareham. In addition to these, there were several other places where evidence exists for markets, mints, or burgesses and other indications of urban status, although each place probably had fewer than 500 inhabitants. They included, Bradford-on-Avon, Bedwyn, Calne, Tilshead, Salisbury, Cricklade, Wilton, Marlborough and Warminster; Frome, Milborne Port, Crewkerne, Milverton, Taunton, Bruton, Langport, Axbridge and possibly also Yeovil and Watchet; and Wimborne Minster.

NEW MEDIEVAL TOWNS

The earliest towns developed on the site of former Roman towns or in a fortified place such as a Saxon *burh* like Wareham or Cricklade where the defences can still be seen. Others developed around important bridges like Bradford-on-Avon, a busy river port like Langport, or on well-used routes such as Marlborough, Milborne Port or Crewkerne; while rich ecclesiastical institutions attracted markets to their gates as Wimborne, Shaftesbury and Salisbury, the latter still within the defences of the Iron Age site on the hill at Old Sarum. To these 'organically' developed towns were added during the period of population growth in the twelfth and thirteenth centuries a larger number of new 'planted' towns, created by bishops, abbots and other large landowners for the profit they would bring. Such towns can often still be recognised by the regularity of their plans, since they were generally created on new sites or on empty land adjacent to an existing village. A successful market town would bring to the lord much greater profits than would come from agricultural tenants, and many lords therefore obtained the necessary royal charters, laid out the new streets and plots and a market place, and hoped to attract craftsmen and merchants to settle there by granting them special rights and privileges as inducements. The wide straight streets, the regular 'burgage' plots (that is the plots laid out for the burgesses or townspeople to establish their workshops, shops and dwellings), with the house frontages onto the street, each extending back to enclose about a third of an acre, and situated along both sides of the street or around the proposed market-place, are still easily recognised. There are too many of such planned medieval towns in the region to mention them all, but good examples include Chipping Sodbury founded during the late twelfth century in a corner of Sodbury parish, with its place-name element 'Chipping' or 'market' giving a clue to its origin. Marshfield, with its classic straight street, and a wide market-place at the east end somewhat constricted by later building, was granted a charter in 1265. In Wiltshire two excellent and easily recognisable examples survive, both created by the bishops of Winchester. One is at Downton, south of Salisbury, founded in 1208 and laid out in a broad straight street along the west bank of the river Avon, away from the older settlement around the parish church on the east side of the river. The wide street of the 'planted' new town of Downton is still called 'The Borough', as is the former market-place of another planned medieval town, Montacute in Somerset. The second, and perhaps best example of all in the region was founded by the bishop of Winchester in 1220 at Hindon on a new site in the parish of East Knoyle. Hindon can never have completely fulfilled the expectations of its founder, for it remained small and still consists of one long wide street lined on either side by what are still obviously the burgage plots of 1220. At Hindon better than anywhere else the whole concept and plan of a new medieval town can still be easily recognised.

29 Hindon, Wiltshire, a planned town created during the early thirteenth century (Photograph: J. H. Bettey)

A few planned towns achieved great success; they soon became important and profitable urban centres and are now large modern places. The two best examples are Devizes and Salisbury. Devizes was founded in c. 1135 and is situated within the outer defences and the park of the Norman castle there. The curving pattern of streets and the shape of the two market-places still reflect the way in which the town was laid out in two stages

30 The Site of the former town of Old Sarum, with the Castle mound and foundations of the Cathedral (Photograph: J. E. Hancock)

around the castle. Most remarkable of all is Salisbury, which was transferred from its hill-top site at Old Sarum to the meadow land below in 1219. The old site was constricted within its Iron Age fortifications which contained both a cathedral and castle as well as the town. Quarrels between cathedral clergy and the inhabitants of the castle, difficulties for townsmen caused by lack of space and shortage of water, all led to support for a move to a new site. The new town of Salisbury was carefully planned and laid out on a regular grid pattern, with a large close surrounding the new cathedral on which work was started in 1220, with parish churches, market-place and the burgage plots arranged in rectangles or 'chequers', and the streets watered from the Avon. The new town was an immediate success and within 20 years there were complaints from the townspeople at nearby Wilton that their market was being adversely affected by their new neighbours. Not all the towns were successful, though. Somerset has several examples of failures, including Stoford, south of Yeovil, where three parallel streets were laid out in the thirteenth century by a ford across the river Yeo and at the boundary of Somerset and Dorset, but the planned town failed to achieve the success hoped for by its founders or to compete with the nearby market at Yeovil, and has reverted to a small village. Another Somerset failure was at Rackley or Radeclive on the former course of the Axe about two and a half miles west of Axbridge. In 1189 Reginald, Bishop of Bath and Wells, obtained a charter from Richard I authorising him to set up a port on the river '. . . that he may make a borough on his own land of Radeclive ... with a market and other free customs and liberties that any borough has that is in our land in England'. The Bishop no doubt hoped to export lead from his Mendip mines through this new port, and for a time the port was indeed a success, for a dispute of 1390 concerning the place mentions cargoes of salt, iron and fish, and barges carrying goods inland along the watercourses of the Somerset levels. Drainage works and other changes in the water-levels may have spelled the end of this port; certainly the site is now beside a small stream and is covered by an apple orchard, giving little indication that it was ever a port or that ships could ever have reached it.

In Dorset is the site of one of the best of all examples of an ambitious plan for a new town which ended in total failure. This was Newton on the southern shores of Poole harbour; it was a project of Edward I and intended as a port from which Purbeck marble, then in great demand, could be shipped. A charter was granted in 1286 providing for two weekly markets and an annual fair, and the new town was planned with a harbour, market-place, church and burgage plots. Merchants were to be attracted by generous privileges. But in spite of royal support and backing, the whole project collapsed and little of the grand scheme was built. Today only the name 'Newton' on the Dorset heathland fringing Poole harbour remains as a reminder of what was intended.

In spite of all the senseless destruction which has occurred in towns during the twentieth century, and the way in which shop-fronts, or even whole buildings, have been ruthlessly demolished in favour of standardised modern replacements, much of interest remains for those who are prepared to look for it. In particular the obviously planned shape and pattern of

31 The market-place at Somerton (Photograph: J. H. Bettey)

streets, the surviving market-places and burgage plots, even the way in which markets and other originally open spaces have been encroached upon by later 'infills', still gives great interest to an exploration of these medieval 'planted' towns. A walk around planned towns such as Montacute, Somerton, Corfe Castle, Weymouth, Wickwar, Thornbury, Hindon and many others reveals at every hand features of interest about the original concept. The observant visitor can consider the way in which the buildings fit the function of the town; the way in which a newly laid out linear town like Chard is related to the original settlement around the parish church at the significantly named Old Town; how the route of the main street of such planned towns as Dunster, Montacute, Somerton and Chipping Sodbury has obviously been diverted out of its original course to take traffic through the new market-place; or the way in which later building in some of the burgage plots, as at Hindon, has created a mass of little alleys and crowded buildings and workshops at the back of and at right angles to the original shops and dwellings which face the street.

LATE MEDIEVAL TOWNS

Side by side with the 'planted' towns, the organic growth of others continued. Some prospered from industrial growth like Castle Combe, Wilton, Pensford and Shepton Mallet, others depended upon a wealthy abbey such as Abbotsbury, Cerne Abbas, Bruton, Glastonbury and Keynsham. The existence of large castles also influenced the development of other towns such as Dunster, Devizes, Corfe Castle, Sherborne, Castle Cary and Taunton. The increase of trade during the twelfth and thirteenth centuries also led to the rapid growth of ports, notably of course Bristol, but also Bridgwater, Watchet, Lyme Regis and Poole.

For the later Middle Ages it is possible to see something of the development of these towns from documentary as well as from archaeological evidence. In particular it is possible to see how the wooden and canvas stalls in the weekly markets gradually developed into permanent shops, with dramatic effects both on the appearance of the town and on the way of life of the inhabitants. At Cerne Abbas a whole row of late medieval timber-fronted houses which stand in front of the former Abbey gateway in Abbey Street were obviously designed as permanent shops facing on to the market place in front of the parish church, and later buildings erected in the middle of the market place are themselves no doubt the successors to the original canvas and wooden stalls erected there. The account books of Sherborne School and of the Almshouses there give considerable detail about the markets during the fifteenth and sixteenth centuries. There are many references to the stalls and shambles erected for traders and butchers, to fees charged for moveable cattle- and sheep-pens, and to the gradual replacement of the temporary stalls by permanent wooden-framed shops with tiled roofs. A taxation list of 1327 shows Frome with over 70 tax-

Two alternative ways by which Man has changed the land in order to settle on it: ABOVE Iron Age encampment at Maiden Castle, Dorchester; BELOW the Abbey at Bath surrounded by buildings of several different periods (*J. E. Hancock*)

Man's ability to make a dramatic impact on the landscape illustrated by two examples widely separated in time. Wansdyke (ABOVE) was probably thrust across the Wiltshire Downs in the early Saxon period; BELOW Almondsbury Interchange near Bristol, where M4 is linked with M5—the area of these roadworks is greater than that of most medieval towns (*J. E. Hancock*)

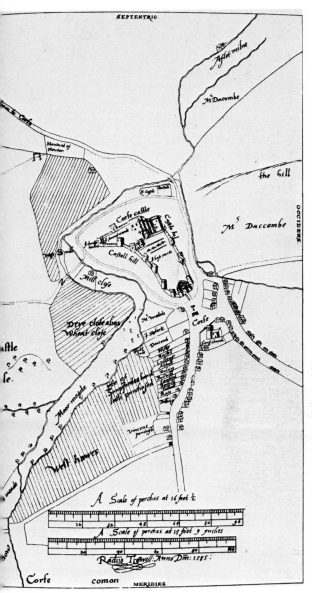

32, 33 Corfe Castle, Dorset (Photograph: National Monuments Record). (LEFT) Plan of Corfe Castle 1585 (Reproduced in J. Hutchins, *History of Dorset*, 3rd Ed., 1861–73)

payers, and in 1392 a rental of the land in Frome belonging to the abbey of Cirencester refers to four named streets, which must indicate the development of an urban lay-out. In Frome the attractive narrow Cheap Street survives as an indication of what some of the streets in these medieval towns must have been like. We also have Celia Fiennes' description of Bristol in 1685 where she found 'the buildings of the town so high, most of timber, the streets narrow and somewhat darkish, because the roomes on the upper storeys are more jutting out soe contracts the streete and light'. A long series of legal disputes about the market places at both Shepton Mallet and Frome during the sixteenth and seventeenth centuries gives copious evidence of the extent of the trade conducted there, and of the stalls set up by butchers, tailors, bakers, corn-merchants and a multitude of others. The disputes also reveal the way in which the temporary stalls slowly gave way to the more permanent shops and how the market places were gradually diminished by successive 'infills' and encroachments. The antiquary John Leland, who travelled through the west country during the 1540s, also gives much information about towns and markets. For example his neat description of Thornbury can still be recognised, '... a letter Y havinge first one long strete and two hornes goynge out of it'; he also adds a comment on the clothing trade of the town. At Lyme Regis Leland described '... a praty market town set in the rootes of a high rokky hille down to the hard shore. This town hath good shippes and usith fisshing and merchauntice. Merchants of Morleys in Britaine [Morlaix in Brittany] much haunt this town'. In west Wiltshire he was evidently much impressed by the flourishing cloth industry in the towns, and wrote of Bradford-on-Avon that 'al the toune of Bradeford stondith by clooth making', and of Trowbridge that it was 'very well buildid of stone, and florisheth by drapery'.

The growth and prosperity of the cloth industry was responsible for the late medieval growth of several towns particularly in Wiltshire and Somerset such as Frome, Croscombe, Steeple Ashton, Corsham and many others. At Castle Combe between 1409 and 1454, 50 new houses were erected, mostly built by clothiers.

A town that presents the visitor with an interesting problem over its plan is Warminster. Here the parish church, on the site of the ancient minster which gives the place its name, stands on the very edge of the town well away from the market-place and the central focus of the town. The reason for this curious and unusual plan is that the church was originally founded to serve a much smaller settlement situated on a slight rise above the low-lying area bounded by two streams. When a massive expansion of the town occurred in the thirteenth and fourteenth centuries, growth took place south and eastwards away from the church; and the market-place, which was to become the greatest corn market in the west of England, was established on higher ground more than half-a-mile from the church, and the centre of the town moved to the area around the market, leaving the church in its present curiously peripheral position. During the fourteenth century a chapel was built in the centre of the town to serve the community around the market place.

FAIRS

It was not only the towns with their regular weekly markets that were important in the economic life of the region. Much business was also done at the numerous annual fairs. Some were held within towns, like the eight fairs regularly held each year in Bristol. Others were set up each year on isolated hill-tops where today it is difficult to imagine the stalls, pens, cattle, horses and merchandise and the crowds that thronged to them. Important three- and four-day fairs were for example held at Whitedown Hill in south Somerset, Tan Hill and Yarnbury Castle in Wiltshire, Woodbury Hill near Bere Regis in Dorset, and Weyhill near Andover in Hampshire. Like the markets, many of the fairs were of no more than local significance, but others attracted custom, both buyers and sellers, from very long distances. John Aubrey commented on the celebrated sheep fair held at Castle Combe on St George's Day (23 April) each year, and called it 'the most celebrated faire in North Wiltshire ... whither sheep-masters doe come as far as from Northamptonshire'. Aubrey also listed other important fairs for sheep, wool, cloth, cheese and other commodities at Wilton, Chilmark, Devizes, Burford near Salisbury, at Salisbury itself and at Tan Hill where 'every yeare on St Anne's Day [26 July] is kept a great fair within an old camp ... The chiefe commodities are sheep oxen and fineries'.

An indication of the distance to which the influence of a fair could extend is given by the partial record which survives of dealings at Whitedown Hill between Crewkerne and Chard during the seventeenth century. People came to this fair from all over west Dorset and from much of Somerset, and a few traders came from much further afield, including some from Wales who brought cattle to sell there. Nothing now survives in the landscape to indicate how important and popular this fair once was, and the site is merely an open space at the entrance to Cricket St Thomas Wildlife Park. Another extremely popular fair was held for three days each autumn on the bare hill-top of Woodbury Hill near Bere Regis in Dorset. Again nothing survives to indicate the former importance of the site. The greatest of all the many sheep fairs in the area was held on the downland at Weyhill near Andover in Hampshire, at the junction of several ancient roads and trackways. Like most of the fairs, this was very ancient and continued to be important in the economic life of the area over many centuries.

A great fair for wool and yarn was held in Somerset each year at Norton St Philip. Like many other west country fairs this one coincided with the patronal festival of the parish church and was held for several days around the feast of SS. Philip and James (1 May). The 'great house or inn called the George' was emptied of much of its furniture and filled instead with the packs and bales of the merchants. As is so often the case, it is the surviving evidence from legal disputes which provides us with detailed information about the fair at Norton St Philip, about the trade conducted there and about the stalls of the traders and the pens for cattle and sheep which were set up all along the highway and in adjacent fields and bartons. Inns like the George at Norton St Philip played an important part in the marketing process, providing meeting-places, exchanges, banking and storage facilities as well as food, drink and lodging. There were no less than 24 licensed inns and alehouses around Shafesbury market in the seventeenth century, and similar large numbers in the other market towns. At Salisbury in 1686 there were sufficient inns to provide accommodation for 548 travellers and 865 horses; Taunton could accommodate 247 travellers, Wells 402, Bath 324, and Bridgwater 142.

MARKET TOWNS DURING THE SEVENTEENTH CENTURY

There are several interesting descriptions of market towns and markets during the seventeenth century and several surviving market-places with their crosses or shelters for the traders. Perhaps the best market cross is at Malmesbury, just outside the gates of the former abbey; another well-known example is at Dunster. Less elaborate crosses mark the sites of many former markets, for example at Salisbury, Martock, Somerton, Cheddar, Stalbridge, Steeple Ashton, Shepton Mallet and elsewhere; and the lock-ups or 'blind houses' where those who misbehaved could be locked up survive in many former market-places, as at Castle Cary, Steeple Ashton, Heytesbury, Shrewton, Pensford and Swanage. One of the greatest corn markets in the region was at Warminster. There was a market at Warminster as early as the thirteenth century, with stalls and shops, as well as an annual fair on the feast of St Lawrence. In the sixteenth century John Leland mentioned the quantities of corn sold there, and in the mid-seventeenth century John Aubrey described it as 'the greatest corn market by much in the West of England', and wrote of how the glovers working in their shops in the town could count 'twelve or fourteen score loades of corn on market-dayes'. In the 1830s Warminster was second only to Bristol among corn markets in the west of England and was especially notable for the quantities of barley sold there. The continuing prosperity of the town and its market is clearly reflected in the fine buildings with their frontages on to the main streets.

Yeovil market was described by Thomas Gerard who lived nearby at Trent in 1630.

The market, of a little towne, is one of the greatest I have seene ... the greatest commodity is cheese, which being made in great abundance in the adjoyninge country is weekly transported hence both into Wilts and Hampshire in very greate quantity; hemp and linen thread are very good chafer [trade] with them too. . . .

Much detail about the trade of the market at Yeovil and about its rapid growth during the seventeenth century emerges from a long and involved dispute there over the profits of the market. The evidence produced bears out Thomas Gerard's remarks about its extent. Until the end of the sixteenth century one beam had sufficed for weighing the produce sold at the market; in 1595 a second beam was needed, and there was clearly an increasing trade in horses and cattle, sheep and pigs, butter, cheese, hemp, linen, leather and corn.

Disputes over rights during the seventeenth century also provide a good deal of incidental information about the market at Shaftesbury. In spite of its hill-top position Shaftesbury is at the junction of a number of important routes, and it is an indication of its former importance that there are still more roads radiating from it than from any other town in Dorset. On market days there was great congestion in the streets; obstructions caused by stalls and standings caused disputes between travellers wishing to get through the town and those attending the market. In 1620, for example, the mayor ordered that some of the stalls in the main street were to be pulled down, since they were 'a great annoyance to the corn market there and to buyers and sellers of corn and victual there and a straitening unto the usual travelling way through the said market and dangerous for travellers and a hindrance to the market men there'. The stall-holders were told to 'goe to places more convenient for uttering their wares' within the town, but many were unwilling to move, 'and ill language giving to the said maior by some of them'. Before long the stalls were back and the complaints and congestion continued as before. It is clear that great quantities of agricultural produce were sold each week at Shaftesbury market. The facilities included a Guildhall in which the mayor's court was held every market day, a market-house where the town scales and weights were kept, a corn market with a bell to ring to mark the beginning of the market, a butter cross 'for all those who sold butter, cheese, eggs, poultry or the like to stand or sitt dry in during the market' and other market crosses for fish, cheese and poultry. Cattle and pigs were sold on the steep incline of Gold Hill, and pens for sheep were erected along the streets. There were also some permanent shops known as 'Chapmen's Standings' which had obviously developed out of the stalls put up for chapmen or itinerant salesmen and pedlars. A great range of wares was offered for sale each week, including, besides agricultural products and foodstuffs, ironware, candles, besoms, gloves, leather and cloth. The town also contained 24 inns and alehouses, most of them around the market-place. For a traveller hurrying on to the West of England, the bustle and crowded streets of Shaftesbury on a market day must have meant hindrance and frustration; but to the farmers of a wide area it was a major outlet for their produce and a crucial feature of their economic life.

TOWN DEVELOPMENT IN THE SEVENTEENTH
AND EIGHTEENTH CENTURIES

From the end of the seventeenth century many of the smaller markets and many of the fairs declined rapidly. In Dorset, for example, there were 22 weekly markets in the county in 1690, but by 1812 the number had declined to 12. The number of fairs also declined greatly, for example, the eight annual fairs of medieval Bristol had been reduced to two by the eighteenth century. There were several reasons for this decline. Better roads, and later canals and railways, made many of the smaller markets superfluous. There were also changes in business methods and the wider use of the sort of regular shops familiar in modern towns. Some smaller markets were engulfed by their larger neighbours; Glastonbury was diminished by the superior attractions of Somerton; Frampton in Dorset was overwhelmed by competition from Dorchester. Plague caused the removal of the cattle market at Highworth to a new site at Swindon; Bath market was for a time moved to Marshfield, because of plague, and there are many other examples. Other small markets failed to recover from fires or from an outbreak of plague; Steeple Ashton, Bere Regis, Beaminster and many other markets suffered disastrous fires during the eighteenth century. The tightly-packed towns of the chalklands were especially susceptible to fire, for the houses were generally close together in the chalkland valley, and in the absence of good building-stone many were built of mud or cob and most had thatched roofs. Fires could therefore spread very rapidly and were a constant hazard. Manorial courts and town councils took what precautions they could, but fires were nonetheless frequent. In 1649 the town authorities at Dorchester bought 'a brazen Engine or spout to quench fire', and at Crewkerne it was the tradition to 'play the Engine' on public holidays, that is to squirt water from the town fire-engine round the market square, a custom which neatly combined rejoicing, horse-play, a holiday spectacle and practice for the town firemen. The churchwardens' accounts regularly contain entries of payments made for 'playing the Engine' as well as for beer for the firemen and grease used to grease the engine and the leather pipes. At Market Lavington and Bere Regis the hooks once used to pull burning thatch off the roofs of houses can still be seen, while Puddletown church still has the canvas buckets which could be used to carry water in case of a fire in the town.

In spite of the dangers, many people were very careless about fire and about naked lights and town records are full of warnings to the inhabitants to be more careful. For example at Amesbury in 1605 the widow Perry was said to 'make her Fyre very dangerous for want of a chimney, her house standing in the midst of the town'. She was ordered not to have any more fires in her house until she had provided a chimney or until 'she hath made a sufficient fier place wherein she maye there make fyer without peryll of sett fier of the whole towne'. Likewise in 1629 the Dorset justices were told of the widow Gaye who lived 'in the heart and middle of the towne of Wimborne Minster and who, though unlicensed brewed great quantities of beer and ale in a flew or chimney made of timber to the great danger of the whole towne'.

Many towns were also very dirty and careless both of adequate sanitation and of a pure water supply. Periodically there were attempts at improvement generally after outbreaks of plague. For example at Amesbury in 1614 the manorial court ordered that all inhabitants should clean the streets before their houses of filth and rubbish and 'make clene all channels to water courses before the house of every of them ... for the common good of the inhabitants, and make and laye together in heaps such durt, soyle and erth fitt to be ridd out of the streete'. Generally, however, the effect of such efforts was very temporary.

The seventeenth and eighteenth centuries also witnessed a massive expansion of some towns in the region. Foremost was Bristol which by this time had become the second port in the kingdom, and for wealth, shipping, industries, trade, churches and buildings was compared by visitors to London. During the seventeenth century Bristol expanded beyond its medieval confines on to the site of the former castle and into the Marsh, and by the end of the century all the open spaces within the city had disappeared as the town expanded and population increased. King Street was new in the 1660s and still contains the fine half-timbered building the 'Llandoger Trow'. In 1673 James Millerd, a Bristol mercer and surveyor, produced his magnificent plan of Bristol, showing in charming and abundant detail the extent of the expansion of the city, its fine buildings, many churches, its great port and varied industries. Early in the eighteenth century Defoe could describe Bristol as 'the greatest, the richest and the best port of trade in Great Britain, London only excepted'. Defoe also noticed the position which Bristol already held and continued to occupy throughout the eighteenth century as the metropolis of the west, whose influence both economic and social extended far into Wiltshire, Somerset and Gloucestershire and across the Severn into Wales. The dramatic increase in the population of Bristol tells its own story of the increasing wealth, prosperity and size of the town. The population was about 10,000 in the mid-sixteenth century; by 1600 it had risen to about 12,000, by about 1670 to 20,000, and by the early eighteenth century to 30,000; by the time of the first census in 1801, the population had reached 63,000. As this expansion of population proceeded the whole appearance of Bristol was altered by extensive building. Fine Georgian town-houses were laid out around elegant squares such as Queen's Square, St James Square and Portland Square. Excellent new streets were built on the slopes of Brandon Hill outside the confines of the medieval town, with houses for merchants such as the Georgian House in Great George Street which is preserved as a typical example of a fine house of this period, with furniture, china, glass and kitchen equipment just as it would have had when it was occupied in the eighteenth century by Charles Pinney, a West India merchant. The centre of the medieval town was also largely rebuilt, with new streets like Orchard Street and Clare Street, and new buildings such as a new Council House, the Exchange of 1742, a new Library and a new Theatre, the Theatre Royal of 1766, now the oldest theatre in the country with a continuous existence. Some idea of the mercantile community of Bristol during the eighteenth century survives in the brass pillars or 'nails' used as tables in the Tolsey, the merchants' meeting place, and which now stand on the pavement in front of the Exchange. Bargains were struck and bills were paid 'on the nail', that is on the brass pillars.

Meanwhile there was growing up at Hotwells and Clifton a fashionable resort where people came to take the waters. The growth of the resort is reflected in the architecture of Hotwells and, to a much grander extent, in the eighteenth-century terraces and crescents at Clifton on the hillside above the river. Dowry Square in Hotwells, which survives with its charmingly varied and elegant houses, was laid out in c. 1720. Some of the houses in Clifton were built by Bristol merchants, notably Clifton Hill House 1747 for Paul Fisher, and Goldney House which became the home of the wealthy Quaker family of Goldney, whose financial interests ranged over many industrial and trading activities. Other buildings were erected to accommodate the fashionable visitors, such as Windsor Terrace, Boyce's Buildings and the Mall, culminating in the spectacular Royal York Crescent of 1810–1820, 'a crescent to beat all crescents'.

In Wiltshire and Somerset town expansion in the eighteenth century was due to the cloth industry. Defoe gives a dramatic account of the way in which the development of the cloth industry led to the rapid growth of Frome during the late seventeenth and early eighteenth centuries; the evidence for this growth can still be seen in this attractive and interesting town. Defoe writing in c. 1720 described how Frome had

... so prodigiously increased within the last twenty or thirty years, that they have built a new church, and so many new streets of houses, and those houses are so full of inhabitants, that Frome is now reckoned to have more people in it than the city of Bath, and some say than even Salisbury itself, and if their trade continues to increase for a few years more, as it has done for those past, it is very likely to be one of the greatest and wealthiest inland towns in England ... Its trade is wholly in clothing ...

Defoe may have exaggerated slightly, but certainly by the early nineteenth century Frome was one of the most populous towns in Somerset, except for Bath. The visitor to Frome can see the way in which the medieval town expanded from the market-place at the foot of the hill by the river, and how growth continued up the hillside. Cheap Street with its medieval atmosphere, and the attractive conduit down the centre full of rapidly-running water, leads on to St John's church and in to Gentle Street, another beautifully curved pedestrian street full of splendid old houses and still paved with stone setts. The evidence of the former prosperity of the town is everywhere apparent. There are the crowded houses in the Trinity area, built to accommodate the cloth workers, the fine seventeenth-century houses of the clothiers such as Merchants Barton south-east of the church and Melrose House in Whittox Lane; Sheppards Barton is named after the largest of the Frome clothiers, and there are elegant Queen Anne and Georgian houses in Willow Vale, King Street, and Vallis Way. The former

34 Gentle Street, Frome (Photograph: J. H. Bettey)

wealth of Frome is also apparent from the fine Bluecoat School and Alms-houses of 1726. Perhaps most notable of all is Rook Lane Congregational church, an enormous building with the date 1707 prominently displayed above the façade. Frome provides a visual textbook of town development and of changing styles, and no visitor should miss the opportunity of exploring its fascinating streets and lanes.

The present appearance of many other towns throughout the region reflects their prosperity during the eighteenth century. Especially notable are Trowbridge with its fine clothiers' houses, Bradford-on-Avon, West-bury, Calne and Shepton Mallet, all of them providing-object lessons in the former importance of the cloth trade and the wealth derived from it. At Wincanton the fine stone houses reflect the eighteenth-century wealth created by the production of high-quality cloth in the town; Taunton, Mil-verton and Wellington have fine buildings erected on the profits of their trade in serges. Away from the cloth-producing areas, the eighteenth-century houses of Poole are evidence of the wealth which came from the Newfoundland fishing industry; amongst many fine buildings in the town are the Guildhall, the elegant Customs House of 1788, the Mansion House and several fine merchants' houses, including Sir Peter Thompson's house of 1749 designed by John Bastard of Blandford Forum, and Beech Hurst of 1798. In these and other large, imposing houses, double-fronted and

35 Eighteenth-century houses at Tory, Bradford-on-Avon, reflecting the affluence which the cloth trade brought to the clothiers of the town (Photograph: Neil Gibson)

of red brick, we see the merchants of the town announcing to the world their success, their wealth and their social status. Similarly we find elegant eighteenth-century houses at Cricklade, around the Green at Calne, and in the wide High Street of Marlborough.

At the other end of the social spectrum, the artisans' houses can be seen at Corsham, Rode, Frome, and perhaps best of all in the terraces rising up the hillside at Bradford-on-Avon—Newtown, Middle Rank and Tory—or in Prospect Square at Westbury. The worst housing for workers which has now mostly been demolished was in the crowded alleys and courts of Trowbridge, houses which must have been a world away from the fine clothiers' houses in the Parade, with their elegant façades and beautifully decorated stonework of c. 1730.

The importance of the clothing industry and the wealth derived from it can be appreciated in the elaborate tombs and monuments which are to be found in scores of parish churches, erected to those who proudly described themselves as 'clothier'. Good examples can be seen at Trowbridge, Bradford-on-Avon, Corsham, Steeple Ashton, Colerne and Beckington. The eighteenth-century prosperity of the port of Bridgwater as well as the later wealth which the town gained from the manufacture of clay drainage-pipes and roofing-tiles is well reflected in its architecture, especially in the fine houses in Castle Street begun in 1723 and in the late eighteenth-century King's Square, as well as in several nineteenth-century houses, hotels and public buildings in the town, notably the Market Hall of 1834 and the Town Hall of 1865. Here too, interesting rows of artisans' houses can be seen, showing in their details changes in fashion and taste, and in what was considered acceptable for the working classes during the late eighteenth and nineteenth centuries. The hemp, rope and sail-cloth industries led to the growth of Crewkerne, Beaminster and Bridport during the eighteenth century, while the manufacture of gloves was important in the Yeovil area, and gloving also contributed to the expansion of Milborne Port, Stoke-sub-Hamdon and Martock. Ports such as Lyme Regis, Bridport, Poole, Watchet and Bridgwater benefited from the export of these manufactured goods, and in addition the Dorset ports were involved in the lucrative Newfoundland fishing industry.

One town in the region—Blandford Forum—was virtually built anew during the eighteenth century after a disastrous fire in 1731. The splendid parish church, town hall and houses round the central market place, are a remarkable and charming example of classical architecture, the work of two local men, the brothers John and William Bastard. The central area of the town has been little altered and well repays investigation on foot.

The eighteenth century saw the growth of Bath as a resort and spa. Throughout the Middle Ages Bath had remained a small and comparatively poor town, confined within its Roman walls. In 1622 the Mayor of Bath could complain to the government '. . . we are a verie little poore Citie, our Clothmen much decayed and many of their workmen amongst us rehoused by the Citie.' The popularity of the Spa grew rapidly during the seventeenth century, however, attracting increasing numbers to take the waters, including Charles II and his Court in 1663, and later the Duke of York and Samuel Pepys. By the end of the seventeenth century there were gravel walks, bowling greens, tennis courts and coffee houses, and Celia Fiennes could describe Bath as 'the town and all its accommodation is adapted to bathing and drinking of the waters and nothing else'; while a few years later Defoe could write sourly that

. . . in former times this was a resort hither for cripples . . . but now we may say it is the resort of the sound, rather of the sick; the bathing is made more of a sport and a diversion, than a physical prescription for health; and the town is taken up in raffling, gameing, visiting, and in a word, all sorts of gallantry and levity.

Under the rule of the arbiter of fashion and behaviour, Richard (Beau) Nash, who became Master of Ceremonies in 1704, Bath became the leading centre of fashion and of fashionable society in the country. Under the impetus of the recommendation of the efficacy of the Bath waters by the physician, Dr Oliver, it also became the leading health resort. The influx of the nobility and gentry led to a massive expansion of the town and

created the opportunity for Ralph Allen to develop the building stone of Combe Down, and for architects such as John Wood the Elder, and his son John Wood the Younger and others to design fashionable houses; between them they created the most architecturally distinguished of English cities and the most beautiful of English spas. The elder Wood's most notable designs were Queen's Square and the Circus; the first was completed by 1736 and the Circus was begun in the year of Wood's death in 1754 and finished in 1758. He also designed Prior Park, Ralph Allen's mansion at Combe Down on the hillside overlooking Bath. John Wood the younger designed Gay Street, Milsom Street and, his greatest triumph, the Royal Crescent built during 1767–75.

The success of Bath in attracting the wealthy and notable in English

36 (LEFT) Civic dignity and amenity: the Royal Victoria Park,
Bath (Photograph: Neil Gibson) 37 (ABOVE) Eighteenth-century elegance in Queen Square, Bath (Neil Gibson)

society during the eighteenth century is apparent from the multitude of
memorial tablets on the walls of the Abbey, recording in elegant prose
and verse the virtues of those who had failed to benefit from the Bath waters
and who are buried there. Other spas were also established in the region,
at Hotwells down the Avon from Bristol, and much less successfully just
outside Melksham during the early nineteenth century, where to the south-
east of the town along Spa Road, three large three-storied houses can be
seen, the remains of the Spa. At the back of one of the houses are the
baths and the pump room.

Notwithstanding all the eighteenth century expansion, however, many
towns remained very small, even though they had a considerable economic
and social importance for the surrounding region. Apart from the weekly

market and the annual fair there was little to distinguish many of the towns of the region from the surrounding villages. Even the craftsmen who tended to be more numerous in the towns continued through the seventeenth and eighteenth centuries to have secondary interests in farming. A Wiltshire linen draper in the eighteenth century held up an order for his cloth because 'a-plenty of apples now imploys many workmen making cider'. Thomas Hardy's picture of Casterbridge (Dorchester) during the nineteenth century remained true of many west-country towns, that

Casterbridge was the complement of the rural life around; not its urban opposite. Bees and butterflies in the cornfields at the top of the town, who desired to get to the meads at the bottom, took no circuitous course, but flew straight down High Street without any apparent consciousness that they were traversing strange latitudes.

SEA-SIDE RESORTS

The development of resorts continued with the growth of Melcombe Regis under royal patronage during the reign of George III, and the expansion of Bournemouth during the nineteenth century. At Bournemouth the first house was not built until 1811 when Lewis Tregonwell, member of a wealthy landowning Dorset family, built, first a house for himself and then an inn and a few cottages for servants, friends and relations. After Tregonwell's death in 1834 a 'marine village' was planned consisting of detached villa-residences set among the pine trees which Tregonwell had planted all over the hillside facing the sea. Not until the coming of the railway did the real expansion of Bournemouth occur, for there were still only 695 people living there in 1851. In the same way Weston-super-Mare grew from a small fishing village in 1801 to become a popular resort with 18,000 inhabitants by 1901; here again the expansion depended upon the railway, as did the development of smaller resorts at Clevedon, Portishead, Burnham and, later still, at Minehead. More detail on this subject will be found in Chapter 6.

NINETEENTH-CENTURY EXPANSION

By the beginning of the nineteenth century the rapid growth of population in the towns of the midlands and the north of England had far outstripped the size of most west-country towns. Only Bristol remained in the front rank although it had already been overtaken by the rapid growth of population in Manchester, Liverpool and Birmingham and had lost a good deal of trade to London and Liverpool. The disastrous slump in both agriculture and the cloth trade after the Napoleonic War meant that there was comparatively little early nineteenth-century building activity in most towns of the region. Not until the heady confidence of the Victorian period are there once more numerous large public buildings and public works, and above all this age saw the coming of the railways, which will be discussed in Chapter 7. Examples of fine buildings of the early Victorian period can be seen in many towns and especially in Bristol. Among several examples are Brunel's Royal Western Hotel of 1837, a fine building which was intended for the accommodation of passengers waiting to embark on the Atlantic steamship services which were started from Bristol in 1838. This building, behind the twentieth-century Council House on College Green, is now sadly neglected. Other examples include Temple Meads station of 1839–40, with its mock Tudor facade and stupendous train shed designed by Brunel with a wooden roof having a span of 72 ft, wider than Westminster Hall, and carried on octagonal iron piers (it lies along the north side of the present entrance to Temple Meads); the Victoria Rooms, now part of the University, were built in 1840; the Guildhall in 1841; the Italianate soap factory in Broad Plain which was later the home of the famous 'Puritan' brand soap and is now a builders' merchants and furniture showroom, was also built in 1841. Various other factories, banks, shops and warehouses survive in Bristol from these prosperous years of the mid-nineteenth century. The massive expansion of Bristol industries during the later nineteenth century—chocolate, tobacco and packaging—is matched by the growth of population and the very rapid expansion in the physical size of the city. The population of 68,000 in 1801 had grown to 159,000 in 1851, and to 330,000 by 1901, and although this growth did not match the massive population explosions of some northern cities, nonetheless it did lead to an enormous demand for new housing and to the creation of vast areas of new suburbs, especially to the north and east of the city, and more and more of the surrounding countryside was swallowed up as Bristol's boundaries were extended. The nineteenth century also saw the completion of Bristol Cathedral which, since the dissolution of the Augustinian Abbey in 1539, had been without a nave and had consisted of chancel and crossing only. In the 1870s and 1880s the nave was built to harmonise with the existing fourteenth-century work; the design was by G. E. Street. But the best known construction of the nineteenth century and the most unmistakeable landmark in Bristol is not a building but the Clifton Suspension Bridge, designed by Brunel in 1829 and finally completed after many difficulties, financial and technical, six years after Brunel's death. It is a magnificent reminder of the man whose work affected Bristol in so many ways from ships to railways.

Other towns also underwent massive expansion of population and physical size during the nineteenth century, and several towns finally broke free from the stranglehold of their medieval boundaries and were able to expand into former agricultural land. Two examples will illustrate this development. Trowbridge, in spite of its importance in the cloth industry and its remarkably fine eighteenth-century buildings, had for long been prevented from expansion by the absence of available building land in the surrounding fields. The result was that during the late eighteenth and early nineteenth centuries the town became very crowded, with dwellings, factories, workshops, dyehouses and the like erected in backyards and huddled closely together. The inevitable result was to create appalling slum conditions in which disease could flourish, and whole areas of the town remained throughout the nineteenth century crowded and unhealthy. These crowded yards and alleys were in marked contrast to the fine houses erected by the wealthy clothiers in the town, and which, according to Sir Niklaus Pevsner, would 'make quite notable additions to the palazzo architecture of ... Verona'.

The second example of expansion is Dorchester. Here the town was almost entirely surrounded by the lands of the Duchy of Cornwall manor of Fordington, and was virtually confined within the lines of the old Roman town. Neither the increase in its population from 1,429 in 1801 to 3,513 by 1851, nor the coming of the railway in 1847 enabled the town to break out of its ancient confines. Not until 1874, when the common fields of Fordington were finally enclosed, was expansion of Dorchester possible. Thereafter the town spread rapidly as middle-class villas and rows of semi-detached houses were built in a great suburban sprawl around the ancient core of the town. The names of the new roads such as Prince of Wales, Victoria, Alexandra, tell their own story of this late nineteenth-century development.

The expansion of the nineteenth-century towns of the region, the coming of the railways, the building of railway stations, the creation of rows of working-class housing, the spread of suburban dwellings, municipal improvements such as parks, gardens, water and gas undertakings, road improvements, schools, civic buildings, museums, art galleries and the provision of new churches of all denominations for the growing population—all these and many other changes can be traced in the buildings and developments themselves. Even the minor public works such as public lavatories, statues, clock-towers, drinking-fountains and horse-troughs tell their own story of civic pride and development; while the names given to roads, streets and public buildings can in themselves reveal much about the date of construction.

The expansion of towns like Bristol, Bath, Weston-super-Mare, Salisbury and many others during the nineteenth century is clearly marked in the street names as well as in the gradual changes in the architectural styles of the houses. In many towns the suburban street and road names provide a roll-call of the events and heroes of nineteenth-century England. In Bristol, for example, the street names recall many of the leading occasions and personalities of the century, and provide admirable dating evidence for the expansion of the built-up area. Readily datable road and street names include Princess Victoria Street, several Queen Victoria streets, streets and roads named after Victoria's favourite residences, Osborne, Balmoral, Sandringham and Windsor; Gladstone, Beaconsfield and Balfour recall Prime Ministers; Wellington, Nelson, Cardigan, Gordon, Kitchener, Trafalgar, Ladysmith, and Balaclava commemorate popular heroes or notable battles. The names of nineteenth-century suburban villas can also be equally informative about their date.

One of the most interesting towns in the region is almost entirely a creation of the nineteenth century; this is the railway town of Swindon which originated when the Great Western Railway Company decided to establish its principal locomotive building and repair works in 1843, near the small market town of Swindon. Soon afterwards the Company began to construct its workshops and to build houses for its workers nearby; these were followed by a church (St Mark 1843–45), a school (1845), a Mechanics Institution (1853–4) and a Methodist chapel (1860). As with all the projects of the G.W.R., Swindon was designed with flair and imagination. The settlement developed into Swindon Railway Village, and is a remarkable example of a planned Victorian workers' estate. In 1851 the population was 4,500, by 1901 the new Swindon of the railway had linked with the old market town of Swindon, and the two together contained more than 45,000 people; four-fifths of the working population were in the employ of the G.W.R.

EVIDENCE FOR THE DEVELOPMENT OF TOWNS

In spite of much destruction and demolition in the twentieth century, a great deal survives in west-country towns to remind the observant visitor of how they have developed over the centuries, and much of the charm and interest of the towns lies in the variety of ways in which their past history can be discerned in their lay-out, defences, buildings, industrial sites and open spaces. This chapter will end with some examples of the sort of things that can be seen and what to look for. Several towns retain evidence of their former defences, none better than Wareham where the great ramparts of King Alfred's 'burh' or stronghold are still clearly to be seen surrounding the town, and where the grid street-plan survives from the late Saxon period. Likewise in Dorchester the line of the town walls is clearly visible, defining the size of the town's Roman predecessor, Durnovaria. At Cricklade the town is surrounded by the square enclosure of the former Saxon defences, and even in Bristol in spite of countless changes and rebuildings, the curve of the streets still follows the line of the former town defences and one of the gateways to the medieval town survives by St John's church.

Several towns in the region developed around the site of a castle, and this is still clearly reflected in their lay-out. In Devizes the curving streets follow the former castle boundaries, and the town is one of the best places to see the way in which various different influences have shaped it over the centuries and how each has left its mark upon it. A major influence was the Norman castle, and the parish church still has substantial Norman work. The shape of the outer defences of the castle can be seen in the curving line of New Park Street, Monday Market Street, Sheep Street, Bridewell Street and others, and the names of these streets also reveal much about their medieval origins. Other influences on the town have included its markets, the canal, the railway and the road-pattern of the district, and all have left visible signs of their influence—especially the canal with its spectacular series of locks. Besides its fascinating lay-out and numerous interesting streets, lanes and alleys, some with surviving medieval, sixteenth- and seventeenth-century houses, Devizes also possesses a fine market place, with a market cross which includes a memorial to an alleged liar, some good inns including the Bear, a Market House, Corn Exchange and numerous interesting buildings of shops, banks, and other premises.

Dunster is still dominated by its great castle, and the modern street plan of Taunton, Bridgwater, Mere, Castle Cary and Corfe Castle, as well as other towns, is obviously influenced by the former existence of a castle. Several other towns developed during the Middle Ages by the gates of abbeys or nunneries, and the influence of the former monastic houses can be seen for example in the lay-out of Glastonbury, Shaftesbury, Cerne Abbas, Sherborne, Amesbury and Keynsham; the cathedrals at Wells and Salisbury had a similar influence upon the respective town plans.

The former crucial importance of the market-place is still evident at Marlborough, Chippenham, Salisbury, Warminster, Castle Cary, Dunster and Thornbury, and can also be traced in towns where the original market place has been constricted by later building, as in Marshfield, Cerne Abbas, Sturminster Newton and Somerton, or in settlements which are now no longer towns at all such as Pensford, Frampton, Steeple Ashton and Sherston, which are now villages but where the former market-places and the surrounding buildings are well preserved and tell us much about their history. Many places also retain their lock-ups or 'Blind houses' as evidence of their former importance; good examples can be seen at Castle Cary, Heytesbury, Steeple Ashton, Trowbridge, Bradford-on-Avon and Warminster.

Almhouses reflecting both the wealth and social concern of their

38 Nineteenth-century shop fronts at Sturminster Newton, Dorset
(National Monuments Record)

founders can be seen in many towns, among them Dorchester, Marshfield, Trowbridge, Sherborne and Bristol. At Sherborne the charming almshouses by the Abbey were founded in 1437 for the support of 12 poor men and four poor women, with a chaplain and a 'housewife' to care for the spiritual and material needs of the inhabitants. This almshouse has had seven centuries of continuous use, and was considerably enlarged during the nineteenth century. In Bristol the attractive almshouses founded by the Merchant Venturers at the end of King Street were built in 1696–99, and continue to exist even though now dominated by enormous office-blocks. On the front wall are the following lines—

> Freed from all storms the tempest and the rage
> Of billows, here we spend our age,
> Our weather beaten vessels here repair
> And from the Merchants' kind and generous care
> Find harbour here; no more we put to sea
> Until we launch into Eternity.
> And lest our Widows whom we leave behind
> Should want relief they too a shelter find.
> Thus all our anxious cares and sorrows cease
> Whilst our Kind Guardians turn our toil to ease
> May they be with an endless Sabbath blest
> Who have afforded unto us this rest.

Evidence of former markets survives in many towns in the form of market crosses, some large and elaborate structures, others no more than a single stone pillar. Crosses may be seen at Cheddar, Somerton, Dunster, Stalbridge, Downton, Salisbury and, best of all, at Malmesbury where the purpose of the elaborate market cross was explained by John Leland in 1540—'for poore folkes to stande dry when rayne cummeth'. The number of inns and pubs which still survive around former market places is a reminder of the important part these institutions played in the marketing process. Sufficient medieval houses survive to enable us to gain some impression of what the towns looked like at the end of the Middle Ages. Notable is the so-called King John's Hunting Lodge at Axbridge, a town-house dating from the end of the fifteenth century. At Cerne Abbas a fine row of timber-fronted houses, evidently intended as shops, runs along Abbey Street from the parish church towards the gate of the former monastery; while at Mells the so-called New Street, running from High Street towards the parish church, was built by Abbot Selwood of Glastonbury in c. 1470 as part of an abortive plan to create a new town there. Two fine inns survive, The George at Norton St Philip and The George and Pilgrims at Glastonbury. Medieval merchants' and priests' houses can be seen at Wells, Salisbury and Wimborne Minster, while in Malmesbury there are substantial remains of medieval town-houses concealed behind later façades or in the cellars of later buildings. Bradford-on-Avon and Frome have excellent examples of seventeenth-century houses for all levels of society, while the evidence of the eighteenth-century prosperity which the cloth trade brought to the region is reflected in the buildings of almost every town, as well as in the nationally famous buildings of the period in Bath and Bristol. The eighteenth- and nineteenth-century inns, town and market halls, corn exchanges and other public buildings of Devizes, Wootton Basset, Thornbury, Westbury, Warminster, Taunton, Salisbury and Dorchester are eloquent reminders of the prosperity and civic pride at this time and, in spite of modern destruction, enough Victorian shop-fronts, elegant town-houses and public buildings survive to provide a wealth of interest and delight for anyone who walks through Mere, Wimborne Minster, Castle Cary, Sherborne, Somerton, Axbridge and a host of other small towns.

High Street, Marlborough

The Church in the Landscape

This chapter will consider the effect of the Church as an institution on the landscape of Wessex, not only in the immediately obvious sense of the major landscape effect of church buildings—parish churches, chapels, cathedrals and the remains or ruins of former monasteries, nunneries and chantries—but also the effect of the Church as an institution, as a great landowner and as an initiator of land reclamation, drainage projects and other enterprises, and as the builder of farms, barns and granges just like any other great estate owner. Church buildings are, however, one of the most ubiquitous and prominent features of the landscape in town and country alike, and it is this aspect of the impact of the Church upon the region that must be considered first.

SAXON CHURCHES AND ECCLESIASTICAL ORGANISATION

Many of the earliest churches were of wood or of wattle and daub. The 'old church' at Glastonbury, which probably dated from the eighth century, was made of wood and was destroyed by fire in 1184. Bede tells the story of St Aldhelm, the first Bishop of Sherborne, and records that the saint was taken ill in 709 at Doulting in Somerset where there was 'a wooden church into which as he was breathing his last he ordered that he should be carried'. No doubt most wooden churches were soon replaced by stone, and in an area such as Wessex which has enjoyed several periods of great prosperity and which possesses a plentiful supply of various good building stones, few early churches have remained unaltered, and, with a handful of notable exceptions, most have been rebuilt several times during the Middle Ages.

There is no doubt that the earliest church-builders consciously sited their churches within or near former pagan shrines, and there are several good illustrations of this in the Wessex landscape. The best is at Knowlton on Cranborne Chase where the parish church, now a ruin, is situated in the centre of a Neolithic ritual monument and some distance from the village. There can be little doubt that the original Christian church on this site was deliberately placed there to emphasise the continuity of

worship and to avoid too great a break with pagan traditions. This policy was encouraged by Pope Gregory the Great who sent St Augustine on his mission to England in 597; in a letter to the Abbot Mellitus, one of the companions of St Augustine, the Pope wrote in 601 advising that the pagan temples should not be demolished and abandoned but rather converted to Christian worship,

Destroy the idols, purify the buildings with holy water, set relics there, and let them become temples of the true God. So the people will have no need to change their places of concourse, and where of old they were wont to sacrifice cattle to demons, thither let them continue to resort on the day of the saint to whom the church is dedicated, and slay their beasts no longer as a sacrifice but for a social meal in honour of Him whom they now worship.

Thus in surroundings which already had powerful and familiar religious associations the people would be won more easily to the new faith. The Pope ended his letter to Mellitus with the astute observation that if a man wishes to climb he should do so by gradual steps and not by leaps.

As well as Knowlton, there are a number of other churches in Wessex which appear to have been established on pre-Christian religious sites. Oldbury-on-Seven church is situated on a hill-top, away from the village and within a circular, prehistoric earthwork, while its dedication to a Saxon saint, St Arilda, is additional evidence of the antiquity of a church on this site. The church at Moreton on the heathland of south-east Dorset stands

94

39 (LEFT) Knowlton Church, Dorset, situated inside a neolithic 'henge' or ritual enclosure (Photograph: J. E. Hancock)

40 (RIGHT) The Saxon church at Bradford-on-Avon (National Monuments Record)

on a large mound which is probably a prehistoric burial-place; and those at both Avebury and Stanton Drew are situated beside the great prehistoric stone circles; at Avebury the church, with its considerable Saxon remains and fine Saxon font, is undoubtedly an early foundation. Roman altar stones are to be found built into the parish churches at Compton Dando and Tockenham, while several other churches make use of Roman materials including Mildenhall and Whitechurch Canonicorum. The parish church at Maiden Bradley is situated on or beside a former Roman burial ground.

In spite of the fact that few churches in the region have survived from the Saxon period unaltered, and that in many all signs of early work have been overlaid by later additions, there are several churches with notable amounts of surviving Saxon work. Among these is the Saxon church at Bradford-on-Avon, one of the most important Anglo-Saxon buildings in the whole country, which may be in part the church referred to by William of Malmesbury as built by St Aldhelm early in the eighth century. At Wareham there are two churches with substantial quantities of Saxon work; at Breamore down the Avon from Salisbury the church retains much Saxon work including a mutilated but still remarkably powerful figure of the crucified Christ and a notable Anglo-Saxon inscription over an arch inside the church, which reads HER SWVTELAD SEO GECWYDRAEDNES DE ('In this place the Word is revealed to thee'). There are many other churches with

Saxon work in their structures or with pieces of sculpture, carved stone-work, cross shafts, fonts or other early work. Notable among these is Inglesham in the far north-east of Wiltshire, which possesses a delightful late Anglo-Saxon sculpture of the Virgin and Child. Carvings of the Green Man, the pre-Christian symbol of vegetable fertility, a figure surrounded by foliage and often with branches and leaves emerging from mouth, nose and ears, are to be found both inside and outside countless churches in the region, from an early town church like St John's, Devizes, or a sophisti-cated late medieval church like St Mary Redcliffe, to the smallest and humblest village churches. Not infrequently the pagan Green Man is to be found incorporated into Christian carvings, as at East Brent, where on the western face of the late medieval tower a series of carvings portraying various religious subjects culminates in a carving of the Blessed Virgin; closer examination reveals that the Virgin's feet rest firmly on the figure of the Green Man. Another notable pre-Christian figure is to be found carved on part of a ninth-century cross-shaft in the church of Codford St Peter. This shows an elegant male figure holding a branch of foliage in one hand and executing a stylised dance. This remarkably lively figure probably represents a spring dance, and the fact that it appears on a cross-shaft is further evidence of the intermixture of pagan and sacred emblems which is so frequently found in west-country churches. Even more remark-able are the male and female fertility figures which survive on several churches in the region. A grotesque female figure with exaggerated sexual organs survives on the church at Oaksey, and male fertility figures may be seen on those at Abson and Fiddington. Many west-country churches also contain carvings from the Saxon and Norman periods depicting beasts, dragons, monsters or pagan symbols such as the tree of life, the signs of the Zodiac or frantic patterns of interlaced scrolls and knots. The persist-ence of all these figures and symbols is a remarkable tribute to the tenacity of these ancient beliefs and superstitions and to the sub-culture of witch-craft, magic and acceptance of the forces of evil which underlay the formal Christianity of the Middle Ages.

The number of churches multiplied rapidly during the Saxon period. At first the missionary activity of the Church operated through 'minster' churches, with groups of priests who were jointly responsible for the spiri-tual welfare of the large areas controlled by each minster. Only gradually were the large territories of each minster divided up into parishes each with its parish church; the process was not complete by the time of the Norman Conquest, and indeed the division of parishes and the creation of new churches went on throughout the Middle Ages. In Dorset the sites of early minsters still retain the element in their place-name such as Char-minster, Iwerne Minster, Yetminster, Sturminster and several others, while elsewhere names like Pitminster, Warminster and Bedminster are a reminder of their origin. Documentary evidence survives for the existence of Saxon minsters at Bruton, Crewkerne, Northover (just outside Ilchester), Taunton and Wells. The church of St John at Frome probably occupies the same site as a monastery dedicated to St John the Baptist founded there by St Aldhelm in the seventh century.

The places within the territories of the early minsters which were regularly visited by priests seem often to have been marked by crosses before churches could be erected. The ninth-century life of St Willibald, written by a nun of Wessex origin, comments that on the estates of many lords there was not a church but only a cross. A number of fragments of pre-Conquest crosses still exist within later churches, for example at Bitton, Ramsbury, Melbury Bubb, West Camel, Colerne and many other places. Gradually churches were built to serve the surrounding areas and the territories of the minsters were split up into parishes, each with its own church. Often churches were built by local lords for their estates which then became the parish, so that in some areas the territorial organisation of the church reflects the early tenurial arrangements in the area. The churches themselves were frequently built near the lord's own house and the church adjacent to the manor house is still a common feature of the region—attractive examples are to be seen at Nettlecombe, Brympton D'Evercy, Chalfield, Mapperton, Binghams Melcombe and many others. We can get some idea of what many of these Saxon churches were like from the substantial survivals in places such as St Lawrence, Bradford-on-Avon, St Martin, Wareham, or Salisbury, although such churches should not lead us to suppose that all Saxon churches were small; some were very large, like the surviving example at Breamore (Hampshire), the Saxon church of Lady St Mary in Wareham which continued in existence until it was demolished by the Corporation there in 1836, or—largest of all—the former great Saxon Cathedral at Sherborne.

For Somerford Keynes, close to the Wiltshire border in Gloucestershire, there is interesting documentary as well as archaeological evidence of the foundation of the church. In 685 Berhtwald, nephew of Ethelred, King of Mercia, granted 40 hides of land to St Aldhelm who was at that time Abbot of Malmesbury. The church at Somerford Keynes incorporates a doorway with an arch cut from a single stone. This may well be part of the original church on that site, built by St Aldhelm for the workers on the new estate belonging to his monastery.

MEDIEVAL PARISH CHURCHES

The five centuries from the Norman Conquest to the Reformation saw an almost constant process of church building, alteration and enlargement, and a very large number of churches were built which continue to be a major feature of the landscape. Examples of small Norman village churches survive in a few places, notably at Winterborne Tomson (Dorset) Culbone (Somerset) or Manningford Bruce (Wilts), but most have been so enlarged, altered or completely rebuilt that little now survives of the earliest part of the structure. Aisles were added, chancels enlarged and roofs heightened during the thirteenth and fourteenth centuries, while in the great spate of church building during the fifteenth and early sixteenth centuries ever larger and finer churches were constructed with wide naves and aisles, soaring pillars to support the high roofs, large chancels, and most impressive of all the elegant western towers which are such notable landmarks and which are an outstanding characteristic of west-country churches, and especially those of Somerset.

Considerable evidence survives from the later Middle Ages concerning the way in which many parish churches in the region were built or enlarged and on the way in which the money was raised and the building work organised. In a few places the churches were rebuilt on a grand scale by one or more wealthy benefactors. The fine church at Wellow is reputed to have been built at the cost of Sir Thomas Hungerford who had been the first Speaker of the House of Commons; North Cadbury church was rebuilt and greatly enlarged at the expense of Lady Elizabeth Botreaux. Steeple Ashton church was paid for by the Long and Lucas families, who were wealthy clothiers there, and there are numerous other similar examples. But the great majority of parishes had no wealthy benefactor, and in such places the enlargements and adornment of the parish churches rested entirely upon the parishioners. It is clear from those places from which churchwardens' accounts survive such as Croscombe, Tintinhull, St Michael's at Bath, Yatton, or St Edmund and St Thomas at Salisbury, that the money was raised by the parishioners themselves through church 'ales', collections, gifts and fund-raising activities, and that building work was arranged and supervised by the churchwardens. A good example is the parish of Dunster in west Somerset where the parishioners decided to add a tower to their church in 1442. The whole project was a communal enterprise master-minded by the churchwardens. The contract survives, made between the churchwardens and a local mason, John Marys. The money was raised by the parishioners both to purchase the necessary materials, stone, timber and scaffolding, and to pay John Marys. It is also clear from the contract that few men were to be involved in the actual building work, for the contract stipulates that if any of the stones was so large that three men could not lift it then the parish was to provide additional muscle-power.

... if there be any stone ... of such quantity that ii men or iii at moste may not kary [carry] hym the said parishe shall helpe hym.

Above all it is the parish-church towers that throughout the whole region dominate the landscape. There can be no doubt that during the latter part of the Middle Ages different parishes vied with each other in the size and magnificence of their church towers. This is true all over the region, but

41 Winterborne Tomson church, Dorset. A good example of a small Norman Church (Photograph: J. H. Bettey)

42 The medieval houses in the Vicars' Close, Wells (National Monuments Record)

43 The fifteenth-century Priest's House at Muchelney, Somerset (Photograph: J. H. Bettey)

is especially the case in Somerset where earlier in the Middle Ages many churches had central towers, but these were demolished and replaced by much larger ornate western towers during the fifteenth and early sixteenth centuries. Today we can only be amazed at the enthusiasm with which small parishes raised the money for these costly structures, and at the skill with which the towers were erected and decorated with intricate carvings, elaborate windows, buttresses and pinnacles, and adorned with statues of the saints. Among the finest Somerset towers are Chewton Mendip, Evercreech, Batcombe, Huish Episcopi, Kingsbury Episcopi, Ile Abbots and Bishops Lydeard, but another dozen examples could easily be added to this list. Wiltshire also has numerous fine towers, notably Steeple Ashton, Bromham, Colerne and others, as well as the incomparable spire of Salisbury cathedral; while in Dorset there are such splendid towers as Beaminster, Bradford Abbas and Wimborne Minster. By the end of the Middle Ages there were few places in the region which were far from a view of one or more of the superb towers, and certainly nowhere that was out of earshot of the church bells. Throughout the whole region the church towers are a constant presence and are without doubt the major single contribution of the Church to the landscape.

The medieval parish churches and their towers not only dominated the landscape of the countryside, they were also a major feature of the medieval towns. At Bristol no less than 18 parish churches were crowded in and around the small area of the medieval town, besides numerous monastic foundations; in Bath and the surrounding area there were numerous parish churches in addition to the Abbey; while such towns as Salisbury, Devizes, Taunton and Ilchester had several churches each, as well as chantries and other religious establishments.

MONASTIC BUILDINGS IN THE LANDSCAPE

Almost equally important in the late medieval landscape were the sumptuous buildings of the numerous religious houses which existed throughout the region. These however, have not survived like the parish churches, and many now exist only as ruins, while for many more their sites retain little to show the extent and magnificence of their buildings. At the sites of several once great monasteries it now requires a powerful imagination to visualise the former extent of their buildings or the impact they must have made on the landscape. The religious houses of Wessex were remarkable for their antiquity, for their wealth and splendour and for their number. Nowhere in the region was more than a few miles from a major monastery or nunnery. Many of these were pre-Conquest foundations like Glastonbury, Athelney, Malmesbury, Shaftesbury, Cerne, Abbotsbury and several more; and by the end of the Middle Ages their great buildings dominated the landscape. The fragments that survive at places such as Forde, Glastonbury, Cleeve, Lacock or Malmesbury remind us of what was lost in the revolutionary changes of the sixteenth century. To take only one example: the great abbey church at Malmesbury, founded in the seventh century, was a landmark for miles around; the church was 240 ft long, with two great towers, one of them surmounted by a spire higher than Salisbury Cathedral. Not only were the monasteries impressive as landmarks, but the needs of the monks encouraged the growth of towns and villages around them, and the activities of the religious houses as great landowners also had a profound effect upon the landscape. The richest of the monasteries and nunneries like Glastonbury and Shaftesbury had estates scattered over several counties, while Keynsham Abbey possessed much land in the surrounding district, many valuable properties, houses, shops and inns in Bristol and extensive lands in Ireland. The evidence of the impact of the monastic landowners upon the landscape is still apparent. Great monastic barns survive at Abbotsbury, Tisbury, Glastonbury, Lacock and Bradford-on-Avon; the fifteenth-century barn at Tisbury is the largest in England, nearly 200 ft long with an enormous thatched roof 1,450 square yds in area, surely one of the most impressive buildings in Wiltshire. It belonged to the nuns at Shaftesbury as did also the barn at Bradford-on-Avon, which is only slightly smaller, at 168 ft long still much larger than most parish churches. The expensive building work engaged upon by the monastic houses meant that they were eager to exploit the resources of their estates as fully as possible. The surviving records of Glastonbury Abbey show the monks farming and managing their estates to the best advantage, with enormous sheep flocks, carefully planned use of the arable lands and a constant movement of stock and produce between various manors, and regular consignments arriving at the great barn at Glastonbury for the use of the monks and lay brothers. The monastery was also involved in lead-mining on Mendip, and played a major part in the large-scale medieval drainage work of the Somerset Levels; during the Middle Ages a large part of the Somerset Levels was controlled by the Cathedral church of Wells, and by the abbeys of Glastonbury, Muchelney and Athelney, and most of the medieval drainage work was planned and carried out by these ecclesiastical organisations. It was the monasteries also that were responsible for coastal reclamation and sea-defences along the coast, and many of the Glastonbury tenants at Brent, Berrow, Lympsham and other places along the coast held their lands during the Middle Ages in return for work on the sea walls and coastal sea-defences. As early as the time of the Domesday Survey in 1086 Glastonbury was one of the richest abbeys in the whole country, and as well as extensive properties elsewhere, owned one eighth of Somerset. This great wealth, which increased during the Middle Ages, is reflected in the massive building work that continued at the abbey right up to the time of the Dissolution in 1539.

The early fourteenth-century Fish House belonging to Glastonbury

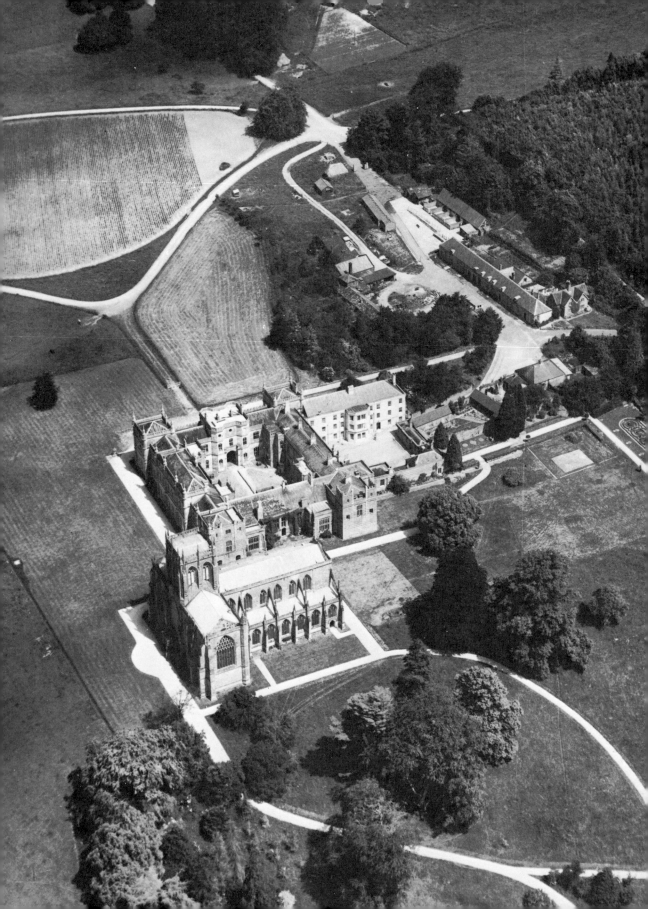

Abbey which survives at Meare is another reminder of the way in which the monks exploited the resources of their estates and affected the landscape. Most of the work on the monastic estates was done by tenants, and certainly in the later Middle Ages the monks did not engage in farming themselves. An exception may have been the Cistercians at Cleeve whose order had a tradition of manual work. As late as the reign of Elizabeth, elderly men who gave evidence in a dispute over some land formerly belonging to Cleeve Abbey, could remember the monks working on some of their own land, they recalled seeing the monks in their white habits working in the fields and remembered especially one incident when

divers muncks of the said Abbey came unto a broomey close [i.e. field infested with broom] parcel of the grange, having eache of them a new paire of Gloves upon their hands and there did pull upp the younge broomes there growing until their newe gloves were well worne and their hands sore with drawing of Broomes.

This may perhaps suggest that the monks were unused to manual work, and certainly such incidents must have been rare in the later Middle Ages, since most of the manual work was done by paid employees and the monks devoted themselves to the services in the monastery church.

OTHER ECCLESIASTICAL INSTITUTIONS AND
BUILDINGS IN THE LANDSCAPE

Besides the parish churches and the monasteries there were also several other ecclesiastical foundations which have had a major impact upon the landscape. The most obvious today are the cathedrals at Wells and Salisbury with their enormous churches and with their associated buildings in the Close at Salisbury and in the Liberty at Wells, the latter including the remarkable Bishop's Palace—the finest of all such buildings in the country—and the incomparable Vicars' Close, a planned street of the mid-fourteenth century, built to house the clergy who conducted the cathedral services. Associated with the cathedral at Wells are two other remarkably interesting buildings, one being the thirteenth-century Treasurer's House at Martock, the other the twelfth-century Canon's house at Horton (Avon), which was enlarged in 1521 by William Knight, an important ecclesiastical lawyer who later became Bishop of Bath and Wells. Comparatively few medieval priests' houses have survived, although as well as those already mentioned, there is the delightful Priests's House at Muchelney (a rare survival of a small fourteenth-century vicarage house); and in Dorset, the Chantry at Trent is a late medieval house intended for the chantry priest, while in the same county two early sixteenth-century priests' houses survive, Abbey House Witchampton, built of brick, and the Priest's House at Wimborne Minster, while a fifteenth-century vicarage survives at Congresbury in Avon.

Especially important in towns were the religious houses of the various

44 The former abbey, cloisters and
site of the town of Milton Abbas,
Dorset (Cambridge University
Collection)

orders of friars, as well as religious foundations for chantries, almshouses and hospitals. Bristol was surrounded by monastic houses, including the priory of St James and the houses of the friars—the Black Friars near Broadmead, the Grey Friars in Lewin's Mead, the Austin Friars near Temple Gate and the White Friars near the present site of the Colston Hall. There were also hospitals in various parts of the town and numerous chantries with their chapels. All these were in addition to the 18 parish churches and to the wealthiest foundation of all, the abbey of the Augustinian canons whose church was destined after the Reformation to become the cathedral of the new Bristol diocese.

At Ilchester there was a Dominican friary as well as an Augustinian nunnery and a leper hospital; Salisbury possessed houses of the Francisans and the Dominicans, and St Nicholas Hospital which still survives as an Almshouse after having been in existence for seven centuries. There was a Franciscan friary at Dorchester as well as a hospital of St John the Baptist and a Leper hospital or 'Lazar house'. Other towns possessed a similar variety of religious institutions. Perhaps the best surviving example of a medieval almshouse is at Sherborne, where the Hospital of St John the Baptist and St John the Evangelist was established in 1437 for 12 poor men and four poor women with a matron and chaplain to attend to their bodily and spiritual well-being. The building with its beautifully preserved chapel and refectory is still used for its original purpose, although it was enlarged and expanded during the nineteenth century. Chantry foundations also affected the landscape, since some had responsibility for the upkeep of roads and bridges. The chantry of the Assumption of Our Lady on Bristol bridge, which had an annual income of £27 6s 0d, was charged with the duty 'to keep and repair the Bridge of Bristol, piers, arches and walls, for the defence thereof against the ravages of the sea ebbing and flowing daily under the same'. In other places also religious institutions or persons maintained roads and bridges. There was a chantry chapel on the bridge at Bradford-on-Avon, while at Chippenham in the later Middle Ages a hermit kept in repair a causeway which led across the marshy land towards Calne, and collected alms from those who used the road.

Isolated chapels on hill-tops or other remote situations were also a prominent landscape feature. The tower of St Michael on the Tor at Glastonbury continues to dominate the whole of central Somerset; and in Dorset chapels survive on the hill-top at Abbotsbury and Milton Abbas, and on the coast at St Aldhelm's Head, while there were formerly chapels on the downland at Cerne Abbas, at Puncknowle and elsewhere.

During the Middle Ages social life in the region was dominated by the Church, and most parishes had Churches Houses or parish meeting-places in which meetings, social gatherings, wedding feasts and church 'ales' or fund-raising activities were held. Many of the late medieval church houses survive, often close to the parish church, and remain attractive features

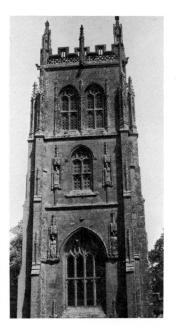

45 (LEFT) The Ham-stone tower of Ile Abbots, Somerset, with its surviving medieval statues (Photograph: J. H. Bettey). 46 (RIGHT) Tarrant Crawford, Dorset. Formerly the site of a nunnery for which Bishop Poore of Salisbury wrote a set of Rules during the early thirteenth century. One of the Rules ordered 'Ye shall not possess any beast, my sisters, save only a cat' (Photograph: J. H. Bettey)

of village centres. Good examples of such church houses are to be seen at Crowcombe and Chew Magna; at Sherborne the church house survives as a long room over a range of sixteenth-century shops in Half Moon Street. Documentary evidence survives for the building of other church houses, like that at Yatton which was built by the churchwardens in 1445 or the church house of St Ewen, Bristol which was built in Broad Street in 1493 and paid for by the gifts and donations of the parishioners. Church houses remained in use until the Puritan changes in church during the seventeenth century, when they turned to a variety of other uses, as schools, vicarages, poorhouses or private dwellings. Some became inns and have therefore remained as central features of the village community, like the former church house at Stoke-sub-Hamdon which is now 'The Fleur de Lis', or the church house which was built near the church during the late fifteenth century at Long Ashton, and which was called 'The Angel'. The Long Ashton church house was built by Sir Richard Choke, who was Lord Chief Justice of England and who is buried under an elaborate tomb in the parish church; in 1495 his son, Sir John Choke, gave the church house, 'The Angel', to the parish in return for an undertaking that regular prayers should be offered from the pulpit for the repose of his soul and the souls of all his family. The house survives and still bears its original name, but is now a public house. A notable example of a pilgrims' *hospice* or lodging also survives at Glastonbury as an inn, the George and Pilgrims, a remarkably fine late medieval building.

Finally, an example of a feature of the medieval landscape which, although not strictly ecclesiastical, was nonetheless inspired by religious devotion and charitable concern, is Maud Heath's Causeway. This runs for four and a half miles across the low-lying claylands of north Wiltshire from Wick Hill to Chippenham. In 1474 Maud Heath, a pedlar woman from Langley Burrell, left property sufficient to create and maintain a causeway across these frequently flooded lands; her causeway survives as a useful as well as interesting component of the landscape.

THE EFFECT OF THE REFORMATION

The Reformation changes of the sixteenth century greatly diminished the impact of the Church upon the landscape; for although the parish church buildings remained, monasteries, chantries and chapels were dissolved and many were rapidly demolished or converted to other uses, while most of the estates of the Church passed first to the Crown and then into various private hands. In many places the new owners were quick to demolish the buildings in order to get the lead from the roofs or to use the stone and timber for other purposes; other new owners speedily converted the buildings into a mansion house. The scale of the destruction is still apparent from the ruins which survive, for example at Glastonbury, Malmesbury or Cleeve, or from the evidence in the landscape of the size and extent of the former buildings, as at Cerne Abbas, Milton Abbas, Amesbury, Hinton Charterhouse or Lacock. The quality of the former monastic buildings is also apparent from what survives, and the effect which the monasteries must have had upon the landscape can be appreciated by the dramatic quality possessed even by the ruins, and by the obviously spectacular sites which were chosen for such religious houses as Malmesbury, Keynsham, Milton, Shaftesbury and several others.

A number of former monastic churches survive as parish churches. At Sherborne the magnificent abbey church was purchased by the townspeople in 1540 and became the parish church in place of the much smaller parochial church of All Hallows which had previously served their needs. Similarly former monastery churches were turned into parish churches at Malmesbury, Milton Abbas and Stogursey. In Bristol the former church of the Augustinian canons became the cathedral of the new diocese of Bristol which was founded in 1542. Bath Abbey church fell rapidly into ruin after the dissolution in 1539, and was not restored for use as a church until after the visit of Queen Elizabeth to Bath in 1574.

Several of the monastic buildings were converted into private residences, and here again the scale and magnificence of the surviving buildings gives some indication of what was lost at the Reformation. This process as well as the dispersal of the monastic lands and the impact on the landscape of the break-up of the great monastic estates will be discussed in Chapter 8; but the spectacularly fine buildings of former religious houses which now survive as private residences at Forde Abbey, Milton Abbas, Cannington, Woodspring, Hinton Charterhouse or Lacock are a constant reminder of the wealth and splendour of many of the west country monasteries and of the effect which they must have had upon the landscape.

THE CHURCH IN THE LANDSCAPE SINCE THE REFORMATION
Church building virtually ceased at the Reformation. During the century before every corner of the region had witnessed major church-building work of all sorts: rebuildings, enlargements, new towers and other spectacular and expensive work. For the next two centuries such work was rarely seen. There are a few examples of new post-Reformation churches: Low Ham near Langport was built, entirely in the Gothic style, during the seventeenth century; it was begun by Sir Edward Hext who died in 1623 and completed after the Civil War by his grandson George Stawell. The former mansion of the Hexts and Stawells has gone, and the church now stands alone in the middle of a field, a remarkable example of a 'medieval' church born out of its time. Wyke Champflower near Bruton was built during the 1620s by Henry Southworth, and is actually attached to his manor house. Several churches also underwent considerable alteration during the seventeenth century, notably at Abbotsbury and Bruton where new or reconstructed chancels were added, and at other places such as Axbridge and Muchelney major work was done on the churches though most was interior work and has, therefore, little impact on the landscape. A few new towers were, however, built during the seventeenth century, for example at Keynsham where the new western tower was built in 1634 to replace a tower at the north-east corner of the nave which had collapsed in 1632, at Chippenham where the upper part of the tower and the spire were built in 1633, and at Midsomer Norton where the tower was built after the Restoration of Charles II in 1660 and contains a niche with a statue of the King.

Rather more churches were built in the region during the eighteenth century. Notable among them were the fine church of St George's, Portland, designed by a local man Thomas Gilbert and consecrated in 1766; Blandford Forum (1733–39) designed by the brothers John and William Bastard and built as part of their rebuilding of the whole town-centre after its destruction by fire in 1731; Hardenhuish near Chippenham, which was built in 1779 to the designs of the great Bath architect, John Wood; and in east Somerset the two delightful churches of Babington near Radstock and Berkley near Frome were built in 1750 and 1751 respectively.

From the seventeenth century onwards the landscape was also affected by the growing practice of erecting gravestones and other memorials in churchyards. Until this time those who had been rich enough to afford memorials were buried inside the churches and their monuments erected there. Churchyards were thus free of obstructions and could be used for all sorts of games and recreations. The custom of erecting gravestones co-incided with Puritan disapproval of many of the games and pastimes that had been held in churchyards, and these were effectively stopped. Church-yard memorials became ever more elaborate, and many were minor works of art as well as often being remarkably interesting and informative. Per-haps the most outstanding of all churchyards in the region is at St Georges, Portland, where there was a long tradition of working in stone and where great care was obviously lavished upon extremely fine headstones which add greatly to the attractiveness of this very interesting church.

From the seventeenth century the Church also made an impact upon the landscape in a new guise, for the various nonconformist churches began increasingly to build their own places of worship. There are now few vil-lages without one or more nonconformist chapels, and in the towns the impact of the large and often ornate chapels is very great.

In Dorset, to take one county as an example, the growing strength and wealth of the nonconformists is to be seen in the size and distinction of the surviving meeting-houses. There are fine early Quaker meeting-houses at Bridport and Poole, large Congregational churches at Lyme Regis, Wareham, Poole and elsewhere, and a distinguished Unitarian chapel at Bridport. The impact which such chapels have on townscapes can be seen from the now-disused Rook Lane Congregational chapel at Frome, the demolition of which would be a major loss to the town. Even in places where the nonconformist chapels are small and not architecturally dis-tinguished they add much to the interest and character of their surround-ings with the greater variety of their styles and their names such as 'Salem', 'Ebenezer', 'Bethel', 'Sion' and 'Bethesda', and the multiplicity of their denominations bear witness to the fervour and rivalry of the different sects. To mention only a very few examples, a delightful Baptist chapel of 1734 survives at Bratton, while at Melksham, Claverham and Long Sutton there are charming Friends' Meeting Houses of the early eighteenth century. At Norton Fitzwarren there is a Congregational chapel and minister's house built as one unit in 1821, while Ile Abbots has a little 'Bethesda' chapel dated 1805. Almost every village could add to the list. Perhaps the most unusual is at East Lulworth, where in the grounds of the now ruined castle are two churches. One is the parish church, the other is a Catholic chapel which was built by the local landowners, the Catholic Weld family, in 1786–87, the first building especially for Catholic worship to be erected in England after the Reformation. It is said that George III gave Thomas Weld permission to build a Catholic place of worship but stipulated that it should not look like a church. The result is a building

47 (LEFT) Churchyard monument, one of the incomparable collection of headstones at St Georges on the Island of Portland (Photograph: J. H. Bettey) 48 (RIGHT) Rook Lane Congregational Church, Frome, 1707 (National Monuments Record)

reminiscent of a piece of eighteenth-century landscape garden ornament, a pantheon or Roman temple.

The period from the late eighteenth century to the end of the nineteenth century saw more activity in church building than any time since the Middle Ages, as the Church of England, the various Protestant nonconformists and the Catholic churches all strove to provide accommodation for the rapidly increasing population, especially in the towns. The townscapes of Bristol, Bath, Salisbury, Swindon, Frome, Taunton and many other places were greatly changed by the addition of new churches and chapels of all denominations. In addition many older churches underwent drastic restoration or in some places were completely rebuilt. For the Anglican churches alone, the figures for church-building and the sums of money spent are staggering. In Wiltshire, for example, between 1837 and 1887, 32 churches were enlarged, 98 were restored, 51 rebuilt and 45 completely new churches erected. One example out of many of individual zeal and generosity was Mary Caroline, Marchioness of Ailesbury, who lived at Tottenham House in Savernake Forest from 1837 to 1879 and was largely responsible for the rebuilding or restoration of nearly all the parish churches in that part of Wiltshire as well as for the building of four new churches. In Dorset between 1840 and 1876 no less than 158 parish churches underwent major rebuilding or restoration, and among many which had very large sums spent upon them were the following:

Sherborne Abbey	£31,715
Weymouth Holy Trinity	£12,050
Wimborne Minster	£10,211
Milton Abbas	£9,000
Weymouth St John	£7,500
Long Crichell	£14,000
Fontmell Magna	£12,000
Corfe Castle	£10,000
Portland St Peter	£8,000
Bere Regis	£5,806

There are many other examples of similar large sums spent upon church buildings and restoration throughout the region during the nineteenth century, evidence both of the wealth available and of the piety and concern for church buildings which was such a feature of large sections of contemporary society.

The church revival of the nineteenth century also led to the building of many schools, vicarages, parish meeting-houses and halls of all kinds and for all denominations, all of which are now an intrinsic feature of the towns and villages. Two developments in church architecture during the twentieth century, both of Catholic origin, have made a dramatic impact upon the landscape of the region. The first is Downside Abbey which was established near Midsomer Norton as early as 1814 and whose fine buildings—especially the great twentieth-century tower 166 ft high, and enormous church—constitute one of the most impressive structures in Somerset, and dominate the whole of that part of the county. The other, more recent development, is the new Catholic cathedral at Clifton in Bristol which is a notable addition to the architecture of the city.

The Wessex region with its large numbers of fine churches and chapels faces in an acute form the problem afflicting the whole country of what to do with those buildings which are no longer required for religious worship or which the congregations can no longer afford to maintain. Imaginative solutions to this problem have been found in a few places where former church buildings have been turned into museums, concert halls, community centres, record-offices or libraries; the use of St Nicholas church in Bristol as a museum of church art or of St Thomas, Winchester, as the Hampshire County Record Office are imaginative examples of such transformations. But far fewer possibilities exist for the multitude of rural churches which may become redundant. A discussion of this desperate problem, which is likely to become ever more acute during the next few decades, is outside the scope of this book, but the dramatic effect on the landscape of town and country alike which the loss of church-buildings will have if they should be demolished is a measure of the importance of the part the Church continues to play in the landscape.

The Coast, Ports and Harbours

The region has a long and remarkably varied coastline, both in Somerset on the Bristol Channel and in Dorset on the English Channel, ranging from the rugged cliffs of west Somerset to the sand dunes and mud flats of Clevedon, Weston-super-Mare and Burnham; or from the sandy beaches of Bournemouth, Poole harbour and Studland to the geological curiosity of the Chesil beach, the great bank of pebbles running from Portland to beyond Bridport. The ports along both coasts have played an extremely important part in the economic life and development of the area, and have exercised an influence extending far inland. The Romans used ports near the modern settlements of Hamworthy in Poole harbour and Radipole near Weymouth to supply their forces in A.D. 43 and 44 when, under the commander Vespasian, they made their rapid and successful assault upon the Durotrigian strongholds in Dorset. Later during the settled period of Roman rule they used the port of *Abonae* at Sea Mills at the junction of the rivers Avon and Trym, north-west of Bristol, for the export of lead from their Mendip mines, and the existence of a Roman temple at Jordon Hill near Weymouth suggests that they may have used a port there also, perhaps at nearby Radipole. The abundant evidences of Roman occupation and activity in Purbeck and around the shores of Poole harbour make it very probable that they also made extensive use of the fine natural harbour at Poole.

Most of the Saxon invaders came into Wessex via the Thames valley and Hampshire, through harbours at Portsmouth and Southampton, but there is some evidence for Saxon landings along the Hampshire and Dorset coast, especially in Christchurch harbour, Poole harbour and at Charmouth in west Dorset. There is no doubt that throughout the Saxon period the rivers flowing into the English Channel—the Piddle, Frome, Stour and Avon—were of great importance as lines of communication, as was also the Bristol Avon, and the ports at the mouths of these rivers were no doubt correspondingly significant in the economic life of the region, although of this little evidence survives.

The third group of invaders, the Vikings, were entirely dependent upon the sea for their attacks upon the region during the ninth century. The first appearance of the Vikings anywhere in southern England came in 790, when a small party landed at Portland and killed the royal 'reeve' and his companions who came to meet them, presuming them to be traders. The really important attacks upon the Dorset coast, however, began in 835 and continued for many years as a major threat to the peace and security of the region. The Vikings also attacked the Somerset coast; they landed near Carhampton in 836 and again in 843, and although they were repulsed at the mouth of the Parrett in 845 their surprise attacks upon the Somerset coast continued to be a menace to the inhabitants. It is the attempts made by King Alfred to provide more adequate defence against these attacks by sea that has left a major impact upon the landscape, in the form of those burhs or fortified strongholds with their surviving massive defences at Wareham, Watchet, and many inland places which were discussed in Chapter 4.

PORTS AND HARBOURS AT THE TIME OF THE DOMESDAY SURVEY

The Domesday Survey of 1086 provides the first clear guide to the ports, harbours and other features of the coastline. In Dorset the boroughs included two ports, Bridport and Wareham, and there was also a large population on Portland, some of whom must presumably have been engaged in fishing and seafaring. Fisheries are also mentioned near Weymouth and at Lyme Regis; while it is clear that the production of salt was an important occupation along the Dorset coast, since salt-pans and salt-workers are named at five places. In Somerset the fisheries named are all inland in the marshy lands of the Levels and along the rivers; of the boroughs only Watchet was on the coast, and we can only conclude that the ports of the county were not especially important at this time. Bristol, however, was obviously a major town by 1086 with an important port and a lively market. This picture is further emphasised by evidence from a few years earlier; St Wulstan, Bishop of Worcester from 1062, had Bristol in his diocese, and was greatly concerned at one aspect of trade from the port, the export of English slaves to Ireland. His successful protests over this trade provide us incidentally with details of the busy port of Bristol and with evidence for the importance of contact with Ireland which was to remain a vital aspect of Bristol trade for many centuries.

THE MEDIEVAL PORTS

During the Middle Ages the ports of Bristol, Somerset and Dorset grew and prospered greatly, largely due to their export trade in wool, cloth, ropes, sailcloth, iron and lead, and to the import of wine. A major share of this trade fell to the port of Bristol, and it was in the interests of its growing trade that the remarkable decision was made to create a new, improved harbour during the years 1239–1247. A fresh channel was cut for the Frome, creating a new confluence with the Avon and providing a deep harbour with good stone quays and a soft bottom for ships to lie safely when the tide was out. This far-sighted piece of civic engineering did much to establish the prosperous port of Bristol during the following centuries; and the Frome still flows along its thirteenth-century channel to join the Avon, although the upper reaches were covered and denied to shipping in the twentieth century, thereby depriving Bristol of one of its most attractive features. The fine medieval churches of Bristol bear dramatic witness to its prosperity as a port during the later Middle Ages and to the wealth as well as to the piety of its merchants.

The sea-borne trade of Somerset also expanded greatly during the Middle Ages, especially through the port of Bridgwater, where exports included cloth and agricultural produce which was sent to France, Spain, Wales and Ireland, while imports comprised wine, fish, oil and luxury goods from the Mediterranean via Spain. By the early fifteenth century Bridgwater was ranked as the twelfth most important port in the country; from which goods were conveyed far inland along the rivers Parrett, Tone and Yeo. Again, the large church and the vestigial remains of the former castle are reminders of Bridgwater's medieval prosperity. Other smaller Somerset ports also shared in the medieval expansion of trade, among them quays at Dunster, Watchet, and landing-places along the Axe, including the port of Rackley founded by the Bishop of Bath and Wells in 1189.

In Dorset several ports achieved prosperity and status during this period. Lyme Regis has no natural harbour at all and owed its existence to the large artificial breakwater known as the Cobb. This was constructed in the late thirteenth century and provided an artificial bay or harbour for ships. The maintenance of the Cobb was to prove a heavy burden for the town, since it was frequently damaged by storms and constantly needed expensive repairs, but it did enable the port to carry on trade with France and Spain and especially with Brittany and Normandy. Bridport is hardly a port at all, lying one and a half miles from the coast, but during the early Middle Ages ships came up the now-tiny river Brit, while later a new port was developed at West Bay on the mouth of the river. Bridport owed its importance to the pre-eminent position it occupied in the manufacture of rope nets and twine. The industry depended upon the hemp and flax produced by the rich soils of west Dorset; Bridport was already famous for these products by the thirteenth century, and its medieval prosperity is reflected in its wide main streets which were the market place of the town. The twin ports of Weymouth and Melcombe Regis also came into existence during the thirteenth century, for although there was a Roman port at nearby Radipole this had ceased to exist by the time of the Domesday Survey and there is no mention of any port in the area. Both Weymouth and Melcombe Regis, facing each other across the narrow harbour, were deliberate, planned creations. Weymouth on the south of

49 The former port of Wareham with the church of Lady St Mary
(Photograph: J. H. Bettey)

the river Wey was founded in 1244, Melcombe on the north in 1268. Wey-mouth on its restricted site between the river and the sea consisted of little more than a single street facing on to the harbour. Melcombe with more room was laid out on a grid-pattern which still survives. Both towns prospered during the years before the Black Death of 1348–49, but both were hit very badly by the plague which started its appallingly destructive course through the country at Melcombe, and wrought havoc in both towns. Inevitably the two towns, separated only by the narrow harbour, constantly quarrelled over shipping, harbour dues, justice and a host of other matters. The bitterness between them continued until in 1571 they were forcibly united by an Act of Parliament, although both kept their separate Parliamentary representation and each continued to send two members to Parliament until 1832.

Poole, which was destined to become the largest of the Dorset ports, also rose to prominence in the thirteenth century, overtaking its much older rival Wareham. The first mention of a settlement at Poole on the edge of the great heath, belonging to the parish of Canford nearly five miles inland, occurs in the late twelfth century. In 1248 William Longespee, Earl of Salisbury and lord of the manor of Canford, obtained a charter for a new town at Poole, and laid out a triangular market place with a town chapel, subsidiary to the parish church of Canford, at its southern end. The port prospered and grew rapidly, profiting from its splendid natural harbour and from the growing demand for Purbeck marble. By the middle of the fourteenth century it had already become the chief port in the county; its growth continued and its importance was recognised in 1568 when it was granted a royal charter giving it the status of a county, with full jurisdiction over its internal affairs. The sixteenth-century and later development of the town was based very largely on the fishing fleet specialising in cod from the distant Newfoundland grounds. This, together with the trade with Newfoundland which accompanied it, brought great wealth and prosperity to Poole so that it far outstripped the other Dorset ports in size and affluence. Ships continued to come up the river to Wareham, however, and this fact can be clearly seen at the former quay which is surrounded by fine buildings, granaries, warehouses and stores. The Newfoundland trade also became extremely important in the economy of the port of Bristol from the seventeenth century onwards.

THE SIXTEENTH AND SEVENTEENTH CENTURY PORTS

Evidence of the state of ports and harbours and of their trade is much more abundant for this period. Ledgers, wills, inventories, accounts and letters of merchants survive, as well as customs accounts and other official records, and there are also numerous descriptions of the ports by travellers. A remarkably detailed picture of the trade of the port of Bristol is presented by the ledger of the Bristol merchant John Smythe, which covers the years 1538–50. The ledger shows that by far the most important commodity exported by Smythe was woollen cloth, much of it coming from clothiers in Wiltshire and Somerset; it was sent to France and Spain. He also exported lead, hides and leather and agricultural produce. His imports included large quantities of wine from Bordeaux, iron from northern Spain and woad and other dyestuffs from Toulouse, the Azores and Genoa. In addition he imported oil for use by cloth-workers and soap-boilers, and occasionally also small quantities of fish and salt. These goods were conveyed in various ships, including his own ship the *Trinity*. The cargoes dispatched in the *Trinity* included goods for many Bristol merchants, for the merchants adopted the sensible policy of consigning their goods to several ships in order to reduce the risk of total loss which might follow the wreck of one of them. Smythe's ledger also reveals the extent of coastal trade between Bristol and ports up the Severn and along the Somerset coast, including Bridgwater, Dunster and Minehead. The wealth which could be acquired through successful trading is demonstrated by John Smythe who, starting with very little, amassed a fortune sufficient to purchase several manors formerly belonging to the dissolved monastic houses in north Somerset and south Gloucestershire, together with the fifteenth-century manor house and surrounding large estate at Ashton Court just outside Bristol.

Details of the Somerset ports during the sixteenth century are given in two enquiries made by the Court of Exchequer in 1559 and 1565 into the collection of customs dues along the Somerset coast. The 1559 enquiry lists seven ports and harbours as follows:

1. Porlock Bay, 'where may ride forty or fifty ships but there is no quay nor safe lying'.
2. Minehead, 'where may lye safflye fyftie ships'.
3. 'A creke called Wachett not mete to charge nor discharge for Shipps cannot have no saffe comminge in nor good Lyinge nor good Rode.'
4. 'A creke for smale Botes called Kylve not fitt to charge nor discharge for that it is very dangerous to come yn or goe owte.'
5. Bridgwater, 'a hedd porte and most mete to charge and dyscharge for all merchaunts'.
6. 'A creke called Hye Bridge not mete.'
7. 'Axwater is a good Ryver where Shipps may come yn and goe owte and also lye saffe without danger, but yet not mete to charge nor discharge for that the port of Bridgwater is so neyre unto yt.'

The 1565 enquiry adds the information that the port of Bridgwater was very busy and much frequented by merchants; that Minehead and Axwater was 'haunted with vessells bringing yn vyctuals, salte, wyne, coale, and wood....'; and that at Dunster, Porlock Bay and Watchet 'smalle boats have use to come yn with salte, wyne, vyctuals, wood and coale, for which purpose they are fit to be continued for the commodytie of the countrye'.

A similar Exchequer enquiry into the Dorset ports in 1608 also reveals interesting details about their trade and above all about the importance of the export trade in cloth. At Lyme Regis, as in other Dorset ports, the main cloth exported was Dorset 'dozens', a coarse narrow cloth made of 'the coarsest wolles growen within the county of Dorset', although higher quality broadcloths, kerseys and serges were also sent from Somerset and Wiltshire to be exported through the Dorset ports. The principal market for Dorset dozens was Normandy and Brittany, where it was stated 'the people are poore and of a Base disposcion and will not go to the price of a good clothe'. A century earlier the antiquarian John Leland had written of Lyme Regis, 'Merchants of Morleys in Britaine [i.e. Morlaix in Brittany] much haunt this town'.

The importance of the cloth trade and the export of cloth continued to dominate the ports of Bristol, Somerset and Dorset throughout the seventeenth century. The port books of the Dorset ports are full of references to various types of cloth: Dozens, Dunsters, Bridgwaters, Barnstaple Bays, Broadcloth, Serges and Perpetuanas. Evidence in a court case at Beaminster in 1627 included the incidental information that there were in the town 'divers cloathiers who doe keepe many people on worke which sell their cloaths to merchants that doe trade them beyonde the seas'. Another case in 1635 included evidence from a man who had made kerseys and bays at Beaminster for the previous ten years; as soon as they were woven he sent them to Lyme Regis to be fulled and dressed by the fuller who then sold them to a merchant for export to France.

In Somerset various types of cloths such as Dunsters, Ilchesters, Tauntons and Bridgwaters were produced all over the county, and not just in the towns which originally gave them their names. From the 1580s medleys or Spanish cloths containing a mixture of English and Spanish wool began to be made in Somerset and rapidly became an important export from ports in the county and from Bristol. The importance of the sixteenth- and seventeenth-century clothing industry, and the wealth produced by it, has left its mark in clothiers' houses and in their monuments in the churches, but it has left little indication in the landscape or little evidence in the ports themselves, for the small ships of the sixteenth, seventeenth and eighteenth centuries did not require elaborate quays or complex equipment for their loading and unloading.

COASTAL RECLAMATION AND LAND DRAINAGE

Throughout the Middle Ages and after, the coastal plain of north Somerset was constantly under threat of flooding and devastation by the sea, in spite of elaborate efforts made to defend it. There are frequent references in the surviving medieval records to piecemeal drainage schemes, and to the building of sea-walls and sluices to allow drainage-water to flow out but to prevent the sea from coming in. At Yatton in 1548 the churchwardens and parishioners sold the silver cross from the high altar of their church and devoted the money to making 'a certain sluice or weir agaynst the rage of ye salte water'.

Along parts of the Dorset coast also there were numerous attempts at land reclamation, especially during the period of agricultural prosperity and expansion in the early seventeenth century. The marshy, low-lying strip of land along the coast at Lodmoor near Weymouth was drained during the 1630s by the landowner Theophilus, Earl of Suffolk, and was made into good agricultural land. Further drainage and sea-protection work in the same area was carried out by the corporation of Weymouth and Melcombe during the 1640s. Evidence of the reclamation work undertaken on Brownsea island in Poole harbour during the same period can still be seen around the shores of the island; this was done by Thomas Bragge, who leased the island from the Earl of Salisbury on condition that he should 'regain embank inclose and defend from the sea' the low-lying land on the island. Large areas of salt-marsh around the shores of Poole harbour were also reclaimed during the early seventeenth century and are listed in detail in a survey of former 'ozie, slubbie or glibsey grounds recovered from the sea' made for the Crown in 1630.

The most ambitious land reclamation project in Dorset was, however, the most spectacular failure. This was a fantastic scheme to drain the Fleet, the area of sea lying between the Chesil beach and the mainland, an expanse of tidal water stretching from Abbotsbury towards Weymouth. During the 1630s a group of Dorset gentry, led by Sir George Horsey of Clifton Maybank near Sherborne, formed a company to drain the Fleet, 'which from time whereof the memory of man is not to the contrarie hath layen under water and over and upon which Meere or Fleetes the sea doth and hath used to ebb and flowe'. Work on the drainage project proceeded very rapidly at first, and large sums were spent by the 'Adventurers', as they called themselves, in constructing a dam to keep out the sea and upon sluices to drain away the water. They were, however, defeated by the inherent impossibility of the task, since the Chesil beach that divides the Fleet from the sea, is itself porous, and during rough weather the sea inevitably poured through and over it, and again flooded the whole area. Sir George Horsey later claimed that he had spent more than £1,000 on the project apart from what had been spent by his partners, and that he had received no profit 'other than some small quantity of Fish'. He also claimed that as a result of the 'Adventurers'' efforts and expenditure part of the Fleet 'was putt into soe good a way of Drayneinge as that a man with boards fastened to his Feet have gone thereupon. . .'. Eventually the whole ill-conceived project collapsed. Sir George Horsey was totally ruined and died, imprisoned for debt in Dorchester gaol, in 1639. His fine house at Clifton Maybank fell into ruin and most of it was finally demolished in 1786; the large porch and part of the front of the house was, however, bought by the Phelips family and re-erected as part of their lovely Elizabethan house at Montacute, where it still displays the Horsey motif of horses' heads.

COASTAL MILITARY DEFENCES

There are comparatively few remains of coastal defensive works surviving from the Middle Ages. In Dorset the great castle at Corfe dominated the whole of the isle of Purbeck and controlled the gap leading to Wareham and beyond. On the island of Portland the curious ruin known as Rufus

50 Weymouth and Melcombe Regis (Photograph: J. E. Hancock)

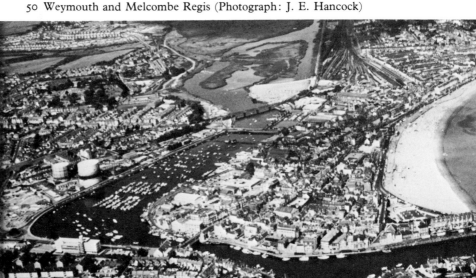

Castle is all that remains of a twelfth-century fortification designed to protect the island and to control Weymouth Bay. In Somerset, Dunster Castle obviously faces out on to the Bristol Channel, and the former strong Norman castle at Bridgwater was clearly intended to protect the port there and the crossing of the river Parrett. Apart from these the coast was undefended by permanent stone defences.

In the sixteenth century some notable additions were made to the coastal defences of Dorset. During the period of threatened French invasion in the 1540s a castle was built on Brownsea island to defend Poole harbour, while to protect Weymouth Bay two castles were built, one at Sandsfoot on the mainland near Weymouth and the other on the shore of the island of Portland. All that remains of Brownsea Castle is now hidden beneath a modern house on the site, and Sandsfoot Castle is a disappointing ruin, but Portland Castle survives intact and is a splendid example of the sort of fortification which Henry VIII ordered to be erected all along the English Channel coast. Built of Portland stone, it presents a squat, curved and strongly fortified series of gun emplacements to the harbour and the bay beyond, reflecting the advances which had been made in artillery during the previous century. The castle is a most attractive and interesting feature of the island.

Coastal defences, strongholds, look-outs and beacons were erected during more recent centuries at various times of national danger, and especially to meet the threat from the Spanish Armada in 1588, from Napoleon, and from German invasion during the twentieth century. Napoleonic and twentieth-century defences can still be seen at various places, for example at Brean Down near Weston-super-Mare and along the Dorset coast at Swanage, Portland, Weymouth and elsewhere; while twentieth-century block-houses, 'dragon's teeth' and other anti-invasion devices are still prominent on many stretches of coast, especially in the isle of Purbeck where military occupation of the area has continued since the Second World War.

DEVELOPMENTS DURING THE NINETEENTH
AND TWENTIETH CENTURIES

The past two centuries have witnessed two main developments in the ports and harbours of the region. One is the improvement in port facilities making the loading and unloading of ships more convenient and enabling the ports to cope with larger vessels; the other is the enormous growth of holiday resorts. Two examples must suffice to illustrate the first development: the changes and improvements in the port of Bristol, and the creation of a great naval base and protected harbour at Portland.

By the beginning of the eighteenth century Bristol was already 'the metropolis of the west of England' with trading connections all over the world. Defoe recognised this during the 1720s when he described it as the greatest, the richest, and the best port of trade in Great Britain, London only excepted. The merchants of this city not only have the greatest trade, but they trade with a more entire independency upon London, than any other town in Britain.

But the facilities of the port did not keep pace with the increase in its trade nor with the growth in the size of ships. Ships coming in to the port of Bristol were still deposited ignominiously on the mud of the harbour bottom twice in every 24 hours as the tide went out, and by the eighteenth century the largest ships did not come all the way up the Avon to Bristol. Many schemes for improving the port were put forward, but not until 1802 was a solution found, when William Jessop was commissioned to construct the Floating Harbour. The Floating Harbour transformed the port, creating a permanent pool in the heart of the city, and enabling ships to float there safely whatever the state of the tide, while a new channel to accommodate the very large rise of the tide was dug along the southern side of the docks, called the New Cut. The new Floating Harbour provided some 85 acres of deep water for ships in the heart of the city; it revolutionised Bristol's dock facilities, as well as transforming the appearance of the city. The enormous work involved both in excavation and in engineering work for lock-gates, bridges and dockside facilities can still be seen by anyone who walks around the now disused city docks, and especially elaborate work can be seen at Bathurst Basin and at the entrance to the Floating Harbour, now somewhat dwarfed under the vast road complex of the Cumberland Basin flyover. The splendid nineteenth-century warehouses which add so much to Bristol's waterfront also make such a walk worthwhile. The Floating Harbour encouraged the expansion of shipbuilding in the port during the nineteenth century, and two of the first ocean-going steamships were built at Bristol, the wooden-hulled *Great Western* launched in 1837, and the *Great Britain* launched in 1843. Both these remarkable ships were designed by Isambard Kingdom Brunel, who was reponsible for so much engineering work and involved in so many projects in Bristol and throughout the west country. The *Great Britain* was the first iron passenger ship and the first to be driven by screws, not paddles; it was also a very large ship for its time, 332 ft long with accommodation for 360 passengers. The ship is now back in the dry dock from which she was originally floated and is being restored to pristine condition; she has rapidly become an established part of the dockside scene and of the landscape of Bristol.

But although the Floating Harbour remains as a remarkable engineering feat, it could not overcome the inconveniences attendant upon the difficult winding journey up the Avon, especially as ever-larger ships were developed during the nineteenth century. The only solution therefore was to develop a new, modern dock at Avonmouth. Development began in 1877, and although Bristol continued to function as a port until the 1970s, the increasing size and convenience of the facilities at Avonmouth, culmi-

51 The Avon Gorge and Clifton Suspension bridge at Bristol
(Photograph: Gordon Kelsey)

nating in the huge Royal Portbury Dock, eventually spelled the end for Bristol as a trading port.

On the English Channel coast at Portland the great naval base and harbour, protected by its enormous breakwater, was constructed during the nineteenth century as a counter to the potential threat from the French naval base across the Channel at Cherbourg. It also provided a safe deep-water anchorage for the new large ships of the Royal Navy mid-way between the two older naval bases at Portsmouth and Plymouth. The decision to establish a naval base at Portland was taken as the result of a Royal Commission which reported in 1844. The necessary Act of Parliament was passed in 1847 enabling the Admiralty to acquire the land for the dockyard and also for the construction of a great military fortification on the Verne, the highest point of the island of Portland overlooking the proposed harbour. The foundation-stone for the breakwater was laid by Prince Albert in 1849 and the main part of the project formally declared finished by Albert Edward, Prince of Wales, in 1872, though since then considerably more work has been done. The breakwaters, together with their entrances, are some three-and-a-half miles in length, and enclose a deep-water harbour of two square miles. The actual work of building the great breakwater was done by convict labour from the prison especially established on Portland for that purpose. The first prisoners arrived on the island in 1848, and the new prison was seen not merely as a cheap method of constructing the naval harbour, but was also an important advance in penal reform. All the convicts were men who had been sentenced to transportation. Before being sent to one of the penal colonies, they were now to spend a year or more at Portland, where they would work in the quarries and on building the Breakwater, and would also receive some education. Good behaviour and hard work at Portland would earn them considerable advantages and eventual freedom when they were taken to the colonies. The new prison which was built on Portland for the convicts working on the Breakwater continued in use until 1921, when it was closed. It was later re-opened as a Borstal Institution. The modern prison on Portland is in the Verne citadel, the former military fortification originally built to protect the naval shipping in the harbour.

As well as developments in ports and harbours, the nineteenth century also saw a vast expansion in some coastal towns of the region through the growth in their popularity as holiday resorts. The beginnings can already be discerned in the late eighteenth century. Lyme Regis became a popular resort for fashionable society from Bath, and is referred to as such by Jane Austen in her novel *Persuasion* published 1818, in which Lyme Regis and the Cobb played a significant part.

As there is nothing to admire in the buildings themselves, the remarkable situation of the town, the principal street hurrying into the water, the walk to the Cobb, skirting round the pleasant little bay, which in the season is animated with bathing machines and company ... are what the stranger's eye will seek...

In 1780 the Duke of Gloucester spent the winter at Melcombe, and soon afterwards built a grand residence, Gloucester Lodge, on empty land to the north of the town. From 1789 George III regularly visited the town, staying at Gloucester Lodge, and the town became dignified as Melcombe Regis. The new-found popularity and rapid growth of the town is reflected in its architecture and in its names. The Esplanade along the shore was started in 1785 and the spread of the resort can be traced through Gloucester Row, Royal Crescent, Chesterfield Place, Charlotte Row, Brunswick Terrace, Frederick Place, Waterloo Place and Victoria Terrace. The popularity of the resort has continued, increasing after the arrival of the railway in 1857, and its growth has gone on in an ever-spreading suburban sprawl through the later nineteenth and the twentieth centuries. In 1809 the crucial debt which the place owes to George III for setting the royal seal of approval upon its qualities as a resort were recognised by an enormous and very effective statue of the King, erected by 'The grateful Inhabitants' and so positioned that it faces up the Esplanade, presiding now over the packed masses of modern holiday-makers on the beach.

Weymouth, facing Melcombe Regis across the mouth of the river Wey, although it has given its name to the modern conurbation formed by the two towns, was for long the poor relation. Its site was more restricted, and lacking the great expanse of beach and shore-line which Melcombe

52 Birnbeck Pier, Weston-super-Mare (Photograph: J. E. Hancock)

enjoys, Weymouth was less fashionable and never acquired the same sort of grand buildings which make the sea-front at Melcombe Regis so distinguished. Much of Weymouth's development has occurred during the twentieth century and the town has expanded inland, or south-west along the hillside to connect with the old settlement at Wyke Regis.

Similar growth in their popularity as holiday resorts was witnessed by Bournemouth and Swanage, while the twentieth century has seen the development of several other small places along the Dorset coast, among them Charmouth, Lulworth Cove and Studland.

In Somerset the development of the seaside resorts came somewhat later, depending more on the railways. The first guide to Weston-super-Mare was published in 1822 but holiday-makers began to arrive in significant numbers only during the 1840s; and Clevedon, although it possesses houses along the sea-front with names such as Adelaide, Brunswick and Clarence, which suggest early nineteenth-century dates, yet its growth as a resort really began with the arrival of the railway in 1847, an arrival which also began the growth of the neighbouring resort of Portishead, and of Burnham-on-Sea farther along the coast.

The amazing growth in the popularity of these resorts on the Somerset coast, their expansion from tiny villages to large towns, and the way in which this depended upon the coming of the railway, and above all the phenomenal growth of Weston-super-Mare, can be seen in the population figures:

	1801	1851	1901
Burnham-on-Sea	653	1701	4922
Clevedon	334	1905	5900
Weston-super-Mare	487	4594	19448

Clevedon is a good place in which to trace the growth of a seaside resort, for it is small enough to walk around quite easily and the buildings of the town show very well the changing styles and designs of the upper- and middle-class houses throughout the nineteenth century. The early nineteenth-century houses are along the sea-front; behind them, spreading up the hillside in roads bearing names indicative of their date, such as Victoria Road and Albert Road, are detached Victorian villas in solid neo-classical style; higher still come the late nineteenth-century semi-detached houses in Gothic or Italianate style, occasionally interrupted by a few mock Tudor or Jacobean houses. The pier, now a sad ruin, was built during the 1860s, and the very solid Royal Pier Hotel with its embattled tower commanding the beach is c. 1870. To cope with the growing population new churches were necessary, and were provided in Christ Church, a very large Gothic building of 1839, designed by Thomas Rickman who did so much to revive interest in medieval architecture and to re-introduce the Gothic style, and who invented the now-familiar names for the different periods of English medieval architecture—Early English, Decorated, Perpendicular; and secondly in St John the Evangelist, designed by one of the greatest of the mid-Victorian church architects, William Butterfield, and built in 1876. A similar progression of styles and fashions in house- and street-names and in architecture can be observed by the visitor who walks away from the beach and sea-front and explores any of the resorts of the region, notably at Weston-super-Mare, Bournemouth or Weymouth.

Unlike the other Somerset resorts, Minehead had for long been an important port with a busy harbour. Defoe referred to it during the early eighteenth century as the best port and safest harbour anywhere along the coast of north Devon and west Somerset, 'No ship is so big but it may come in, and no weather so bad, but the ships are safe when they come in'. Minehead's trade was with Wales and Ireland, particularly in the export of serges, and it also sent ships to Virginia and the West Indies, and throughout the seventeenth and eighteenth centuries carried on a thriving trade in the export of herrings to the Mediterranean. The trade with Ireland was especially important, and as early as the sixteenth century John Leland had commented, 'The town is exceeding fulle of Irish menne'.

Industries, Roads, Canals and Railways

Several industries have been of major importance in the economic life of the region in the past, and have left substantial remains in the landscape. Chief among these is the woollen-cloth industry which for several centuries made Wessex one of the chief industrial areas of Britain. The extremely important medieval cloth trade, to which towns like Bristol, Marlborough, Frome, Bradford-on-Avon, Salisbury and many others owed their early growth and prosperity, has left few surviving evidences in the landscape. This was essentially a hand industry, with few industrial buildings. The great medieval innovation in the industry was the introduction of the water-powered fulling-mill. Fulling was the process of thickening or felting the cloth by treading or 'walking' on it, or beating it with hammers in water, and the mechanisation of this important and laborious process from the twelfth century onwards was one main reason why during the later Middle Ages the industry left the towns in favour of the river valleys where water-power could be used, and where often the sites of former corn-mills could be adapted for fulling. There is documentary evidence for a fulling-mill at Taunton in 1219, and by the fourteenth century they were widespread in Somerset; in Wiltshire evidence has been found for more than 30 fulling-mills which were in existence before 1500. But they are comparatively short-lived buildings, and successive enlargements, alterations and adaptations over the centuries have left few structural remains of the early mills. Undoubtedly many later mill-buildings occupy sites which were in use from the thirteenth or fourteenth centuries, and many mills once used for fulling have since been converted to other uses, but of the early examples in Wiltshire, only Harnham Mill just outside Salisbury retains a substantial part of its medieval structure which dates from about 1500.

A reminder of the former importance of fulling in the cloth industry is preserved in place-names; the west-country word for fulling was 'tucking' and 'tucking mill' survives as a place-name in river valleys all over the region, while Tucker, Fuller or the earlier occupation of Walker are common surnames.

53 A small part of the many sites of prehistoric timber and brushwood trackways which are remarkably preserved in the peat
of the Somerset Levels (Photograph: J. E. Hancock)

54 Crawford Bridge, Spetisbury, Dorset. A medieval
bridge over the river Stour (Photograph: J. H. Bettey)

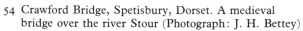

Apart from the fulling-mills, the medieval woollen-cloth industry had no distinctive buildings, for the other processes of spinning, weaving, washing and drying were all done by hand and needed no special buildings. From the sixteenth century onwards, however, there is far more evidence of the industry surviving in the landscape. Most attractive are the clothiers' houses, of which fine examples survive at Shepton Mallet, Croscombe, Bradford-on-Avon, Trowbridge and many other places. Often such houses also have the remains of former workshops attached to them, although until the introduction of powered machinery from the time of the Napoleonic wars, much of the spinning and weaving continued to be carried out in cottages all over Wessex, on simple equipment such as the spinning wheel and the hand loom. John Hooker's description of Devon in c. 1600 would have equally well applied to Somerset, Dorset or Wiltshire.

... wheresoever any man doth travel you shall fynde ... [at every cottage] the wyfe, the children and the servants at the wheel spinning or at theire cardes cardinge the wool, for by such commoditie the common people doe lyve.

Earlier, John Leland, who journeyed through west Wiltshire in c. 1540, had been greatly impressed by the scale and importance of the woollen-cloth industry. He wrote of Bradford-on-Avon that 'Al the toune of Brade-ford stondith by clooth making', and of Trowbridge that it was 'very welle buildid of stone, and florishith by drapery'. Leland made similar comments on most of the towns of west Wiltshire and also of many of the little towns and villages of the eastern and north-eastern parts of Somerset, as for example, of Pensford on the river Chew where he wrote that 'It is a praty market townlet occupied with clothing' and 'The towne stondith much by clothing', or at Chew Magna 'There hath beene good makyng of cloth yn the towne'. Leland also noticed an early example of a woollen-cloth factory. This was at Malmesbury, where William Stumpe, whom Leland described as 'an exceding rich clothiar', had purchased the whole site and buildings of Malmesbury abbey from the Crown at the Dissolution. Stumpe had built a mansion for himself inside the abbey, and had filled '... every corner of the vaste houses of office that belonged to the abbay ... with lumbes [looms] to weve clooth yn'.

Besides the later fulling-mills, numerous other mills and workshops survive from the period after the introduction of machinery, and are to be found all over the region. First water-power was used, and later steam-power was introduced to drive spinning and weaving machinery. Former dye-houses, wash-houses and drying-stoves also survive in several places, notably in west Wiltshire. The woollen-cloth industry has left its mark on innumerable villages in Wiltshire and Somerset like Corsham, Steeple Ashton, Pensford, Beckington, Croscombe and Rode; this shows in their evident former prosperity, in the magnificence of their parish churches, in the fine clothiers' houses and in the cottages erected for the workers. In Somerset a good example is the village of Nunney, where there are fine examples of former weavers' cottages, where a modern estate is named after the Flower family who were leading clothiers in the place, where the late medieval prosperity of the village is reflected in its fine parish church, and where near the striking, moated, medieval stronghold, Nunney Castle, there survives the 'pavement' by the river which was used for washing wool and beside which there was a dye-house. In west Somerset reminders of the former importance of the cloth industry survive in the fine parish churches, including the church at Spaxton near Bridgwater with its remarkable bench-end showing the clothier with the tools of his trade; and in the evident former prosperity of towns such as Wellington, Milverton, Wiveliscombe and others, in the ports of Minehead, Watchet and Bridgwater from which the finished cloth was exported, and in the yarn-market which survives at Dunster. John Leland's description of Frome c. 1540 emphasises its dependence upon the wool and cloth trade, and the prosperity which this brought,

... there be dyvers fayre stone howsys in the towne that standy the most by clothinge ... a metly good market ... a goodly large paroche church in it, and a ryght fayre spring in the churche yarde that by pipes and trenches is conveyde to dyvers partes of the towne ... a stone bridge of fyve arches ...

The area to the west of the town of Frome was developed during the seventeenth century by the Yerbury family, who were prominent clothiers.

Likewise in 1578 the inhabitants of Chard, in an appeal for help after a disastrous fire, emphasised their dependence on cloth,

Whereas within the town of Chard a great and profitable trade hath of a very long time been used in making of woollen cloths to the benefit of our whole realm and especially of all the inhabitants of the County of Somerset, to whom the same town hath been a great aid by employing many a thousand poor people within ten miles compass in working the said trade ...

The cloth from the Chard area was exported through the Dorset ports, especially Lyme Regis, to Bordeaux and La Rochelle.

Fine examples of former cloth-mills and associated buildings survive in many places, for example at Dunkirk Mill, Freshford, in Westbury, Staverton, Melksham and elsewhere. But above all it is at Trowbridge and Bradford-on-Avon that the extent of the industrialisation and mechanisation of the cloth industry can best be appreciated. Trowbridge still possesses a great concentration of former steam-driven mills, especially along the river Biss, and enough survives to show why the town was fondly described during the early nineteenth century as 'the Manchester of the West', and to justify its description by a modern historian of the cloth trade and its buildings as 'the only true factory town of the western industry'. Among many others especial mention may be made of the fine buildings of Castle Mill at Trowbridge, Abbey and Greenland Mills at Bradford-on-Avon and the nearby Staverton Mill which is now a milk-processing factory. Because of their great size and height these factory buildings still make a significant impact on the landscape; their effect when they were first built must have been much greater when there were few if any other buildings of comparable size. Trowbridge also possesses an interesting small building constructed of perforated bricks, standing over the river Biss just upstream from the Town Bridge and the lock-up. This is the only surviving local example of a 'handle-house' where the teazles used for raising the nap on the cloth were dried after use. In Melksham the remains of two drying-houses or 'stoves' survive in which the wool was dried after being scoured to remove dirt and grease. Another interesting building associated with the cloth industry can be seen at Keynsham. This is Albert Mill on the river Chew, a fine building which still has two water-driven wheels and was the last working logwood mill, used for grinding imported logwood or dye-woods from which dye was extracted for dyeing woollen cloth.

Other textile industries have been important in the region and have left their mark on the landscape. In south Somerset and west Dorset the locally-grown flax and hemp gave rise to the sailcloth and linen industry of East Coker, Crewkerne, Beaminster, and elsewhere, and to the rope, twine and net industry of Bridport. Former workshops, factories and ropewalks used in these industries remain in many of the towns and villages of that area; indeed, the industries continue in some places, having successfully adapted to new methods and new materials, including man-made fibres. The silk-weaving industry also enjoyed considerable prosperity during the eighteenth and nineteenth centuries and among other places, it was important at Gillingham and Sherborne, at both of which former silk-mills survive. At Sherborne, by a logical progression the mill once used for silk is now employed in the spinning and manufacture of fibre-glass fabrics. Lace-making has been important at Blandford Forum, Chard and elsewhere.

QUARRYING

Quarrying has also left its mark on the landscape of many parts of the region. The quarries at Box, Dundry, Doulting, Chilmark and Ham Hill, for example, have been used from medieval times and earlier, and the stone is to be found in churches and houses over a wide area around each quarry. In addition there were numerous local quarries which supplied stone to their immediate neighbourhoods, and one of the delights of a journey through any part of the region is to see how the stone used in buildings, walls and hedges changes every few miles, and to observe the varying qualities, colours and textures of the different stones. Dorset possesses two quarries which have enjoyed national and even international fame and importance—Purbeck and Portland. The great period of popularity of

Purbeck stone was the thirteenth century, when polished shafts of Purbeck marble were much sought after for church buildings all over England and abroad. The stone was also extensively used during the Middle Ages for effigies, fonts, coffin-lids, and sepulchral monuments of all kinds. The chief centre of the industry was at Corfe Castle, dominated by the great royal fortress, though the quarries extended over the whole peninsula. After the Reformation the demand for the stone for ecclesiastical purposes ceased, but it continued to be quarried for houses, roofing-tiles and paving-slabs. Daniel Defoe in the 1720s commented on the use of Purbeck stone in London for 'paving court-yards, alleys, avenues to houses, kitchens, footways on the sides of the highstreets, and the like'. In the nineteenth century the stone was again in demand for church restorations and for new churches built in the Gothic style.

The stone from the Island of Portland does not seem to have been extensively used in the Middle Ages, though some was used locally, and there are isolated references to its use in London at the Tower and on London Bridge, and at Exeter Cathedral, in the fourteenth century. The amount of stone quarried seems to have been quite small, and it is significant that Leland, who gives a long account of what he saw on Portland, does not mention quarries. It was during the seventeenth century that the really extensive use of Portland stone began. It was used on the Banqueting House at Whitehall and on repairs to old St Paul's before the Fire. After the Fire of 1666 the stone was chosen by Wren for the new St Paul's and for many of the new City churches, and it gained enormous popularity. The demand continued throughout the eighteenth and nineteenth centuries and stone was exported by sea to a great many towns in the British Isles and was also used on the Continent and in America. By the early nineteenth century it was estimated that more than 25,000 tons of stone were being exported annually from the quarries. During the nineteenth century great quantities of Portland stone were also used at the Royal Dockyards at Chatham, Portsmouth and Devonport, as well as being used by convict labour on the Island to construct the massive breakwater and harbour for naval shipping there. In the twentieth century new building techniques have led to a considerably reduced demand for stone, though quarrying continues on the Island. Stone was also quarried elsewhere in Dorset, notably at Sturminster Newton, Marnhull and Long Burton, and at Upwey and Preston near Weymouth. The industry has been, after agriculture, one of the most important employers of labour; and at times, notably during the thirteenth and nineteenth centuries, the quarrying, finishing and shipping of stone from Dorset has been by far the most important industrial activity in the county.

Notable also were the quarries on Mendip, at Doulting, Dundry and elsewhere; and the quarries of Bath stone which acquired a great importance during the eighteenth century when they were exploited by Ralph

Allen to provide building materials for the expansion of Bath itself as a fashionable spa, as well as for new houses and churches in Bristol and elsewhere. Much of the best Bath stone came from Hazelbury quarry near Box in Wiltshire, and it was this stone which was used during the Middle Ages for many of the churches and monasteries in the area, including Malmesbury, Stanley Abbey, Bradenstoke Priory, Lacock Abbey and Monkton Farleigh Priory. It was also used during the sixteenth century for Longleat House, and for many of the manor houses of north and west Wiltshire. In the south of Wiltshire the most important quarry was at Chilmark, and it was stone from Chilmark and from the nearby quarry at Teffont Evias which was used for Salisbury Cathedral, and for many other churches and houses in that area, including Wilton House. The building of the Wilts. & Berks. Canal and the Kennet & Avon Canal and later, the coming of railways, gave a great impetus to the quarries of Wiltshire, and enabled stone from Box to be dispatched to London and all over the country. The search for Bath stone was extended below ground by mining, and created the great network of tunnels and underground workings which exist today around Corsham.

MINING

The landscape of the region has been affected by several different mining activities. The oldest of these is undoubtedly the lead-mining on Mendip which had been important before the coming of the Romans, since one of the reasons for the Roman conquest of Britain was to secure control of the mines. The ore on Mendip has been worked at depths of more than 200 ft, and over a large area of the Mendip plateau, although Roman activity was centred at Charterhouse. The Mendip mines declined in the face of foreign competition in the nineteenth century, although there were attempts to continue the industry by re-smelting the slag left by earlier miners which, because of the inefficiency of earlier methods, still contained substantial quantities of lead. The eventual end of these operations and the closure of the mines not only brought to an end a very long period of metal extraction, but also spelled the death of the curious laws and customs which governed mining on Mendip. The area had been divided into four Liberties, each under a Lord to whom one-tenth of the produce went, and the actual working of the mines was governed by the complex customs of each Liberty. The industry, together with the associated working of calamine ore for zinc, has made a great impact on the landscape: spoil-heaps and old workings locally known as 'gruffy ground' are to be seen all over Mendip, as well as the evidences of the nineteenth-century re-smelting works in the form of dams and ponds, ruined stacks and horizontal 'chimneys' or flues, and the heaps of slag associated with the work.

The best place to see the evidences of this former highly important lead-mining industry and the later activities in extracting lead from old spoilheaps is undoubtedly at Charterhouse-on-Mendip, where extensive remains survive—ranging from a Roman amphitheatre used by the Roman miners to nineteenth-century re-smelting flues—and where the shiny black slag (the waste from the re-smelting) is everywhere to be seen. At Smitham Hill, overlooking East Harptree and the Chew Valley, the tall chimney of another re-smelting works is a prominent feature of the landscape. Lead and zinc extraction also gave rise to the Bristol brass industry which was of great importance during the eighteenth and nineteenth centuries, and of which former mill buildings survive in various places, especially along the Chew Valley south of Bristol and at the Warmley Brass Works built by William Champion in 1746. Mendip lead was also the basis of the lead-shot manufacturing industry in Bristol. The black slag blocks which were the waste product of the industry may be seen in many buildings and garden-walls in Bristol and the surrounding district.

Iron was mined at various places in Wessex. The most notable deposits of iron-ore were in the Brendon hills; these had been worked from early times, but their real importance came in the nineteenth century when Brendon ores were found to be especially suitable for the Bessemer steel-making process. Evidences of this industry survive in the landscape, notably in the form of tramways, inclined-planes and former railway tracks by which the ore was taken out for shipment to South Wales. Brendon Hill village and the hamlet of Gupworthy grew up during the nineteenth century around the Raleigh's Cross mine to house the miners, many of them Cornishmen who sought fresh work in Somerset as the Cornish tin- and copper-mining industry declined. Iron was also mined at Frampton Cotterell and Temple Cloud in Avon, and at several places in Wiltshire including Dilton Marsh near Westbury and Seend near Devizes.

Coal-mining has left prominent evidence in the landscape of several parts of Avon, notably around Midsomer Norton and Radstock, the former forest of Kingswood, north-east of Bristol, and around Nailsea. Remains of former collieries survive at many places, including Old Mills colliery at Paulton, Pensford, Kilmersdon colliery and Writhlington colliery. The spoil-heaps produced by the industry are widespread over the area of the former north-Somerset coalfield and some indication of the size of the industry may be gained from the fact that in 1900 there were 83 collieries at work in the district; all have now closed. Coal also gave rise to several other associated industries in the Bristol area, notably the glass-making industry of Bristol and Nailsea, but also soap-boiling, pottery, brick-making, and the brass- and copper-working industries.

OTHER INDUSTRIES

Other industries which have made a major imprint upon the landscape can be dealt with briefly. They include the pottery industry and the manufacture of bricks, tiles and clay pipes, which has led to the extraction of clay on the Dorset heathland, both for export in vast quantities and for use in the surviving Poole pottery industry. Dorset clay from around Poole harbour and Wareham was used by the Romans and continued to be worked throughout the Middle Ages. The trade grew rapidly during the sixteenth century and by 1600 there were, for example, 30 brick- and tile-makers living on the heath at Kingston Lacey, and the manorial records of the area are full of complaints about potters who dug great holes to extract clay and who cut turf and peat on the heaths without licence. Later there was a considerable export trade in clay for tobacco pipes and pottery from Poole. John Hutchins, writing in 1773, says that 'Nearly 10,000 tons [of clay] are exported annually to London, Hull, Liverpool and Glasgow, etc., but the most considerable part to Liverpool for the supply of the Staffordshire potteries and to Selby for the use of the Leeds potteries'. This extraction of clay, with its tremendous effect on the landscape of the Dorset heath, has continued and is still a major factor in the economic life of the county. Clay for tobacco pipes was also extracted at several places in Wiltshire, and John Aubrey in the seventeenth century commented on the importance of this trade, particularly at Amesbury—'The best [pipes] for shape and colour . . . are made at Amesbury. They may be called chimneys portable in pockets, the one end being the hearth, the other the tunnel thereof'. Bridgwater bricks and tiles have long been famous, and Bridgwater clay drainage-pipes have played a significant part in land drainage and in agricultural improvement over large parts of south-west England. Agricultural engineering and other industries dependent upon or associated with farming have also been and still are very important in the region, such as food-processing, cheese manufacture, tanning and glove-making. During the nineteenth century firms such as Brown and May of Devizes and Reeves of Bratton became known nationally for the production of agricultural implements, and together with other firms such as Eddisons of Dorchester were large-scale producers of steam-engines and steam-ploughing equipment. The proximity of the railway also contributed greatly to the growth of Swindon as a centre of the engineering industry. The local production of malting barley has meant that the brewing industry has also been very important, and maltings and breweries make a major impact upon townscape at Frome, Devizes, Bristol, Trowbridge, Dorchester and Blandford Forum.

A good place in which to see surviving evidences of industrial activity over a long period is at Kimmeridge on the Dorset coast. Here the Romans worked the black shale to make ornaments, decorations and even furniture. During the sixteenth and seventeenth centuries the Clavell family who owned the lands there attempted to exploit the resources of their estate and engaged in a succession of projects. They dug alum and copperas (used in dyeing) from the lands near the coast and evidences of this work survive in earthworks, in remains of former tramways and in place-names. Next

55 Town Mill, Gillingham, Dorset, built in 1769 as a silk mill (Photo: J. H. Bettey)

56 The Barge Inn, Seend, Wiltshire on the Kennet & Avon Canal (Photograph: Edward Piper)

57 Fiddleford Mill near Sturminster Newton, Dorset. The doorway bears the following inscription dated 1566: 'He thatt wyll have here any thynge don, Let him com fryndly he shal be welcom, A frynd to the owner and enemy to no man, Pass all here frely to com when they can. For the tale of trothe I do alway professe, Miller be true disgrace not thy vest If falsehod appere the fault shal be thine, And of sharpe ponishment think me not unkind, Therefore to be true yt shall thee behove To please God chefly that liveth above'. (National Monuments Record)

they set up a project to produce glass using as fuel the oil-bearing shale which is to be found along the coast and which can be burned, although in burning it emits a dense black smoke and a foul smell. Evidence of the glass industry survives in the form of a pier built by the Clavells to transport their products. Both the alum and glass projects foundered because of legal actions brought against the Clavells by those who had secured monopolies from the Crown for the production of those commodities. The Clavells therefore turned to the production of salt from sea water, again using the oil-bearing shale as fuel. Evidences of this work can also be found along the coast. During the nineteenth century the potential of the area was again exploited when a French company extracted oil from the shale which was shipped from a pier, the remains of which survive; the oil was used to light the streets of Paris. Finally in the twentieth century an oil-well has been sunk on the cliffs and is one of the most productive inshore oil-wells in the country, its small pump and tanks making very little impact upon the landscape of this quiet part of the Dorset coast.

Paper-making has been important in various parts of the region, especially around the slopes of Mendip, where a surviving paper-mill remains at Wookey. Another paper-mill on the Box brook at Bathford continues to make the high-quality thin paper used for printing Bibles. Evidences of the former importance of the paper-making industry can be seen in surviving mill buildings, of which a good example is at Sherborne, near Litton in the Chew valley. This is an appropriately named site, for Sherborne means 'clear stream'—which is of course precisely what was required for paper-making.

Another industry which acquired a national reputation and has left prominent remains in the landscape was the manufacture of edge tools by the Fussell family of Mells. The family began producing edge tools and other farming equipment during the 1740s; their business expanded rapidly, and soon spread into neighbouring valleys and villages wherever water-power was available to drive the mills and grind-stones. The remains of this formerly important industry are to be seen in the valley bottoms all around Mells in the mills, mill-ponds, managers' and workers' houses and in the worn-out grindstones to be found topping walls. Most notable evidence of the former prosperity of the industry survives in the form of Chantry church, which was built for their workers by the Fussell family and consecrated in 1846 to serve a new parish carved out of the old parishes of Whatley, Mells and Elm, whose populations had been swollen by edge-tool workers.

During the nineteenth and twentieth centuries a number of other industries have been established in the region whose buildings have made a major impact upon the landscape. These include the tobacco and chocolate industries in the Bristol region, rubber-manufacture at Melksham and Bradford-on-Avon, footwear manufacture at Street, the chemical industries at Avonmouth, and the gas and electricity industries. The latter has resulted in the most modern intrusion on the landscape of the region in the form of the two nuclear-power stations, one at Hinkley Point on the Somerset coast, the other at Oldbury-on-Seven, and the nuclear research establishment at Winfrith on the Dorset heathland. Another notable landmark for many miles around is provided by the tall chimney of the Westbury Cement Works.

ROADS

One of the remarkable features of the west-country landscape is the complicated network of early roads and trackways which can still be traced; many of them are amongst the earliest roads in Britain. Ridgeways cross the high downlands of Wiltshire and Dorset, among them the Great Ridgeway coming from Berkshire across the Marlborough Downs to Stonehenge and beyond into Dorset; the Harrow Way from the Hampshire Downs across Salisbury Plain, again running past Stonehenge; the Ox Drove Ridgeway which runs from near Shaftesbury right across Dorset to Lambert's Castle, a hill-fort just over the Devon border; and the South Dorset Ridgeway from Hampshire across southern Dorset and on into Devon—this early route, like the others, is marked along its whole length by barrows and other prehistoric monuments. In the Somerset Levels several elaborate timber-built trackways made of carefully-laid hazel, birch and brushwood and dating from the Neolithic period have been discovered, roadways which enabled prehistoric travellers to cross to the various 'islands' then existing amid the undrained marshlands. This complicated system of roads and trackways, covering the whole region, existed for many centuries before the coming of the Romans, and is an important piece of additional evidence for the considerable population and the economic importance of prehistoric Wessex.

The Romans added a further major dimension to this existing complex road-pattern. The new roads built by the Romans were themselves part of the process of conquest, for they enabled rapid troop movements to be made, while their sheer size, width and technical excellence, as well as the forced employment of vast numbers of native labourers in their construction, must have brought home forcibly to the inhabitants of Wessex that they now had new and energetic masters who meant to stay and rule over them. Many evidences of the Roman road-system survive in the landscape, and the routes of many Roman roads are still being used by modern traffic, while others serve as minor roads, bridle-paths and footpaths. The Fosse Way, the great road from Exeter to Lincoln, is still the modern highway for many miles between Ilchester (*Lindinis*) and Bath (*Aquae Sulis*) and on to Cirencester (*Corinium*). Much of the modern road between Ilchester and Dorchester (*Durnovaria*) follows the route of the Roman road; while many of the modern roads around Marlborough are of Roman origin. Dorset possesses several well-preserved stretches of Roman road, among them Ackling Dyke, the road south from the Roman predecessor of Old Sarum. One of the best examples of Roman road in Britain, running straight across the downland parallel to the modern road to Dorchester, the great highway on its raised causeway is one of the most remarkable and evocative monuments of Roman rule in Wessex.

After the departure of the Romans in the fifth century, the Saxon settlers avoided the Roman roads and placed their settlements away from them, so that today the route of the Fosse Way, for example, has few villages along its length, though there are whole strings of villages set about two miles on either side. The Roman roads continued as an important feature of the Saxon landscape, however, as is shown by the fact that they were so often used to mark parish boundaries.

There was little systematic road-building between the Roman period and the coming of the turnpikes in the eighteenth century, although the slow, gradual growth of economic activity and consequently of road traffic through the Middle Ages meant that roads and bridges had to be maintained so as to be at least passable for laden pack-horses. Many fine medieval bridges survive, and for example in Wiltshire there are medieval bridges at Castle Combe, Combe Bisset, Harnham, Milford, Hazelbury Plunkett and elsewhere, while there are medieval causeways at Chippenham and Lacock.

Across the chalk downlands travellers chose the easiest routes and those least plagued by mud and potholes, so that roads tended to become very wide. Early in the eighteenth century Defoe encountered a difficulty which must have been very common for travellers across the downs: he wrote that

Shaftesbury is fourteen miles from Salisbury over that fine down or carpet ground, which they call particularly or properly Salisbury Plain. It has neither house or town in view all the way, and the road which often lyes very broad, and branches off insensibly, might easily cause a traveller to loose his way.

There were no signposts and Defoe would have found it impossible to find his way had it not been that

there is a certain never failing assistance upon all these down for telling a stranger his way, and that is the number of shepherds feeding or keeping their vast flocks of sheep, which are every where in the way, and who, with very little pains, a traveller may always speak with....

Most of these wide downland roads have either disappeared or have become grassy tracks. One of the principal objections to the enclosure of open commons and downland was that travellers would be confined to the narrow limits of new roads laid out between hedges, and that the cost of the upkeep of these narrow roads would be a severe charge on the parishes through which they passed.

Work on parish roads was frequently done unwillingly and inadequately. Quarter Sessions accounts and travellers' memoirs are full of descriptions of bad roads, dangerous bridges and of the difficulties caused to horses and carriages. For example in 1627 the Dorset justices of the peace were told of the bad condition of

the high waie leadinge from the Burrough and Markett Towne of Dorchester in the said countie to the Towne of Waymouth and Melcombe Regis through the whole parish of Broadwaie, especially the lane neare the church of the said village which is so bad that Travellers that passe that waie with carriages either on horsebacke or in carts cannot passe that waie without greate danger. . . .

There are countless similar examples, and complaints about damaged, dangerous or inadequately maintained bridges. In 1687 the notable traveller Celia Fiennes journeyed from Salisbury to Bath via Warminster, and of the road beyond Warminster she wrote

. . . thence to Berkley, 5 mile a deep clay way; we passed over a common of some miles length on a narrow Causy [causeway] that a Coach can scarce pass, all pitched with slatts and stones, our Coach was once wedged in the wheele in the stones that severall men were forced to lift us out; its made only for Packhorses, which is the way of carriage in those parts; the Common is so moorish [marshy] their feete and wheeles would sinke in, so no going there'.

The roads of Wessex were revolutionised by the coming of the turnpike system during the eighteenth century. The turnpikes imposed a new logic on the old haphazard routes and brought sweeping changes to methods of road-building and maintenance. The process began with an Act of Parliament for the turnpiking and improvement of some miles of road in and around Bath in 1707, and this was quickly followed by many other turnpike acts. By the early nineteenth century the Bristol Turnpike Trust was the largest in the country with some 180 miles of road in its care and with a high reputation for its standards of maintenance; this reputation was enhanced in 1818 by the appointment of John Loudon McAdam as Surveyor. In Dorset there were no less than 25 turnpike trusts which controlled some 500 miles of road; all were set up between 1750 and 1780 and all had ceased to operate by 1883. From 1753 a similar network of turnpikes was inaugurated in Somerset, while in Wiltshire the improvement of the roads following the introduction of turnpikes can be traced in the increased speeds achieved by the coach services such as the London–Salisbury and London–Devizes, London–Bath coaches. In 1771 their average speed was 7.4 mph, by 1836 road improvements had enabled this to be increased to 9.6 mph, or by nearly 30 per cent. John Billingsley in his *General View of the Agriculture of Somerset* 1798 also commented on the effect of the introduction of turnpike roads,

Before the turnpike roads were established, coal was carried on horses backs to the distance of fifteen or twenty miles from the collieries; each horse carried about two hundred and a half weight. Now one horse, with a light cart, will draw ten hundred weight, or four times more than the horse could carry: Can an insignificant toll be put in competition with this saving?

The turnpike era has left many relics in the landscape. The roads themselves continue to be used by modern traffic, and the improved routes laid out by the turnpike surveyors are still in use. Large numbers of the picturesque toll-houses survive, as do also many of the distinctive and decorative milestones and parish boundary-stones erected by the Turnpike Trusts. The toll-boards of some trusts, giving details of the charges levied, can still be seen in museums, like the board from Bagstone Gate tollhouse at Rangeworthy which is preserved in the Bristol City Museum. Many of the former turnpike inns also survive beside the modern roads, like the inn at Old Down near Shepton Mallet, the King's Arms at Calne, the King's Arms at Dorchester, the Ship at Mere or the inns at Sherborne, Hindon and elsewhere which still have signs announcing that they have post-horses for hire. In the same way many of the road bridges in Dorset still have an early nineteenth-century notice fixed to them which threatens anyone who damages the bridge with transportation for life. On Salisbury Plain above Edington the now disused route of the former Bath-to-Salisbury turnpike can still be followed as a trackway for many miles across the downland, still marking the passage of each mile with its distinctive milestones.

The progress of road improvement has continued during the twentieth century with ever more lavish by-pass and road-widening schemes, and culminating in the construction of the great motorway network, the most revolutionary change to affect road-transport since the Roman roads. The dramatic impact of the motorways on the landscape is to be seen at many places, in the great bridges and especially in the bridges across the Severn and the Avon, and in the Almondsbury interchange occupying an area of 80 acres—much larger than most medieval towns—at the point where motorways from London, the Midlands, Wales and the West of England converge.

THE CANALS
The period during which turnpike roads reached the peak of their importance and profitability coincided with the heyday of the canal system. The rivers of the region had for centuries been widely used for transport— the Parrett and Tone in Somerset, the Severn, the Avon from Bristol to Bath and the Avon from Salisbury to the sea. During the eighteenth century these facilities were improved and extended. As early as 1664 an Act of Parliament was passed for making the Avon navigable to Salisbury and the Wylye to Wilton; the Bristol Avon navigation to Bath was improved in 1727; and there were improvements in several other rivers. Major canals in the region included the Kennet & Avon, the Wilts. & Berks., the Somerset Coal Canal, the Bridgwater & Taunton, as well as several

schemes for canals which were never actually started or were only partially built, like the various proposals made for a link between the English Channel and the Bristol Channel. Both the Bridgwater & Taunton and the Somerset Coal Canal were of great economic importance for several years. During the peak of its activity during the 1830s and 1840s the Bridgwater & Taunton canal was carrying annual loads of more than 70,000 tons, mostly of Welsh coal, while the Somerset Coal Canal was very important in enabling coal to be got easily away from the mines in north Somerset and conveyed to Bristol and Bath as well as to London via the Kennet & Avon canal. The Somerset Coal Canal was in fact the most profitable and successful of all the canals, and continued to be prosperous until the 1870s, when it succumbed like the others to competition from the railway. The most remarkable canal however, and the one which makes the greatest impact on the landscape, is the Kennet & Avon. It was begun in 1794 and completed in 1810, to carry through-traffic between Bristol and London, via Trowbridge and Devizes. Until the opening of the Great Western Railway in 1841, the Kennet & Avon Canal, 57 miles long and with 106 locks along its length, was of great importance and tremendous economic benefit to the region through which it passed. Within a few years of its completion it was carrying over 300,000 tons of goods a year, but it could not compete with the railway and it was sold to the Great Western Railway Company in 1852; carriage on the canal continued until 1873. Among the many spectacular features of the Kennet & Avon Canal the following are outstanding: the bridges and aqueducts near Bath, especially the Dundas Aqueduct, 150 ft in length, which takes the canal over the Avon valley and is one of the finest examples of civil engineering in the region; the pumping-stations at Claverton and Crofton; the locks at Bath and, most notable of all, the great flight of 29 locks near Devizes, which raised the level of the canal 237 ft, and remains as a great tribute to the energy, optimism and engineering genius of those who planned and built the canals. The pumping-engines at Crofton on the Kennet & Avon are of special interest. They were designed to raise water to the highest part of the canal where it crosses the high land of Savernake forest near Great Bedwyn, 401 ft above the source of the river Kennet. The oldest engine was built by Boulton & Watt and installed in 1812; this has been restored to working order and is one of the oldest working steam-engines in the world, still doing the job for which it was originally built.

The effect of the canals must not be over-emphasised, for they were very localised in their impact, and many parts of the region had no waterways at all. But places within easy reach of the canals were supplied with coal, stone for roads and buildings, bricks, slate, timber, salt and manure, all at a much cheaper rate and in far greater abundance than would have otherwise been possible. Not all of this was pure gain, for the canals began the process, later completed by the railways, of breaking down the old regional traditions of vernacular building using local materials which generally fitted snugly into the landscape, and instead made universally available the far less attractive but cheap brick, slate, clay tiles, and galvanised iron. The canals also for the first time made it easily possible to send large quantities of corn, cheese, butter and other farm-produce out of the rural areas, and greatly extended the available markets. They therefore had the same sort of effect on the agriculture of the few areas affected as the railways were later to have over a much wider area. This was especially the case with the Kennet & Avon canal. A pamphlet issued in 1788 urging the scheme for 'extending the navigation of the rivers Kennet and Avon' had argued that by the building of the canal

The price of carriage of coals and all other articles will be greatly reduced; the estates of gentlemen and farmers will be improved at much easier expense by the introduction of free-stone, timber, brick, tile and other building materials; lime, peat-ashes, and manure of all sorts. They will find new markets for the produce of their farms and estates: corn, malt, cheese, and other great productions, will meet with a ready and cheap conveyance to the great marts.

All this proved to be true, for the canal enabled Wiltshire farmers easily and cheaply to supply Bristol and Bath in one direction, and Reading and London in the other. Cobbett in 1826 commented sourly on the sight of the canal at Devizes,

The great channel through which the produce of the country is carried away to be devoured by idlers, the thieves and the prostitutes, who are all tax-eaters in the Wens of Bath and London.

THE RAILWAYS

The impact of the railways was enormous, much more widespread and dramatic than that of the canals, but the complex story of the various schemes, the rival companies, and the projected routes has already been recounted in many books and need not be told again here. The major effect upon the landscape, however, can be illustrated by brief reference to what is perhaps the most important line in the region, the Great Western Railway from Paddington to Bristol. This railway, 119 miles in length and planned by the Company's engineer, Isambard Kingdom Brunel, was opened in June 1841. Brunel's achievements include the bridges over the Thames, the Sonning cutting, the creation of the new town of Swindon and the great railway workshops, the major impact upon Chippenham with the great embankment west of the town and the splendid viaduct which takes the line over the town, the series of tunnels, cuttings and embankments which mark the western part of the route and include the famous Box tunnel—two miles long with its spectacularly fine entrances— Bath station and its approaches which, together with the bridges and other features in the vicinity, were made in a style designed to suit the dignity of Bath. At Bristol, Brunel created the elegant Royal Western Hotel for passengers who had arrived by rail to embark on the Atlantic steamship services started in 1838. Brunel's Bristol terminus, Temple Meads, was his finest station, with an elaborate Tudor-style façade and an enormous train shed with its 72-ft-span roof; this is the most important and dramatic terminus station surviving from the early railway era.

The expansion of the railway network proceeded very rapidly; indeed, in view of the amount of earth-moving, bridge-building, tunnelling and engineering work involved, not to mention the enormous financial backing required, the progress is nothing short of staggering. The railway reached Taunton in 1842, Salisbury had its railway by 1847, Westbury by 1848 and Frome in 1850; the Southampton to Dorchester railway was completed in 1847. In 1857 the Wiltshire, Somerset and Weymouth line opened. This had been under discussion and construction for several years, and the final route was from Westbury through Yeovil and Dorchester to Weymouth. The building of this line raised interesting examples of concern for the landscape and for the preservation of ancient monuments. The railway company was forced to cut a 700-yd long tunnel at Frampton so that the railway would not spoil the view of the landscaped parkland of Frampton Court through which it passed, and when it became known that the line threatened the hill-fort at Poundbury and the Roman amphitheatre at Maumbury Rings, both just outside Dorchester, a public outcry was raised. As a result the company were forced to tunnel under Poundbury and to make a sharp turn in the line in order to avoid Maumbury Rings. The famous Somerset and Dorset railway, which ran through superbly beautiful countryside and was later to inspire great affection in its passengers, began operating 1862, at first from Burnham-on-Sea to Poole, thus linking the Bristol channel and the English channel. In 1874, the Somerset and Dorset line from Bath to Bournemouth was established and provided a through route from the Midlands to the Dorset coast.

The railways had a profound effect both upon the landscape and upon the social and economic life of the region. The coming of a railway to a town brought prosperity, industry, business and increased population; equally dramatic was the effect upon those towns to which the railways never came, for most of them rapidly declined, markets ceased to be held and population dwindled. Upon agriculture the railways also had a tremendous impact, bringing new equipment, new breeds of cattle and sheep, artificial fertilisers, drainage-pipes, building materials and other supplies, and making possible the cheap, rapid transport of farm produce. The most far-reaching effect was in opening up a vast new market for liquid milk which could now be sent to the towns. The railways virtually killed the local small-scale production of butter and cheese in favour of the liquid milk trade, and also encouraged growth of wholesale milk companies such as the Anglo-Swiss Condensed Milk Company (later Nestlé Company) which opened at Chippenham in 1873. The railways soon became the

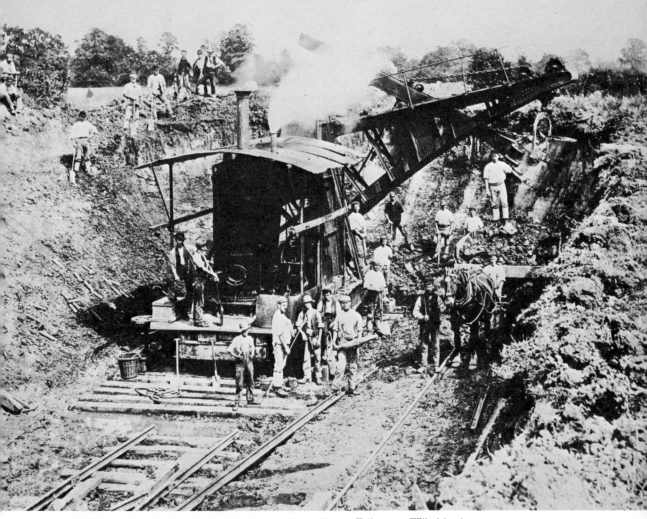

58 Excavating the London to Westbury railway line at Edington, Wiltshire in 1890 (Photograph: Alan Andrew)

essential life-line of the dairy farmers of the region, while on arable farming their effect was equally marked, for they made possible the distribution of cheap imported foodstuffs and especially cheap wheat from the prairies of Canada and the United States, and thus played an important part in the great depression in English agriculture (especially arable farming) during the last quarter of the nineteenth century.

The rapid rise of the railways to a position of vital importance in the economic and social life of the communities they served has been followed in recent years by an equally dramatic decline. The now familiar sight of demolished stations, disused bridges and viaducts, and of deserted tracks disappearing under vegetation, is a reminder of the transitory nature of much land-use and of even the most dramatic of human endeavours to exploit the landscape.

59 The ruins of the Hungerford's great castle at Farleigh Hungerford
(Photograph: Neil Gibson)

The Great Estates

No account of the development of the landscape of Wessex would be complete without some discussion of the crucial effect which the great estates and great landowners have had upon so much of the region. Wessex has traditionally been dominated by great estates—those of the Crown, the Duchy of Cornwall, Oxford and Cambridge colleges, the lands of the colleges of Winchester and Eton, and the estates of the aristocracy and gentry; all these have had an immense influence upon the appearance of the countryside. The country house with its spreading, well-wooded parkland is the most widespread and characteristic landscape feature of the whole region, and the great estates have affected the development of the landscape in many other ways. This is apparent even to the most superficial observer in the multitude of obviously planted woodlands, carefully landscaped vistas, estate villages, farms and cottages, and in the monuments to great landowners which appear on so many hill-tops and which dominate so many of the churches of the region. The great houses like Dunster, Hinton St George, Montacute, Melbury, Wimborne St Giles, Longleat, Badminton, Lydiard Tregoze and scores of others, were sustained by rents from farms and manors scattered over the whole region, and the effects of the dominance of the great landowners are writ large upon the landscape.

LAND OWNERSHIP

The extent to which land ownership in the region was concentrated into a few hands was clearly demonstrated by the enquiry made into the ownership of land in England made by order of Parliament in 1872–73 and published as *Return of Owners of Land* in 1874. For the first time since the Domesday Survey of 1086 precise figures were available concerning the possessions of landowners and the size of their estates. In the *Return* both Dorset and Wiltshire are shown among the counties with the highest concentration of vast estates of more than 10,000 acres. In both counties no less than 36 per cent. of the total area was occupied by such great estates, as against a national average of 24 per cent.; Hampshire and Somerset were both below the national average for the area occupied by such estates:

in Hampshire they accounted for 21 per cent. of the total area of the country, and in Somerset 20 per cent. Hampshire, however, was among the highest of the English counties in the proportion of its total area occupied by estates of from 1,000 to 10,000 acres, with a proportion of 38 per cent. against the national figure of 29 per cent. The figures for the other counties were Dorset 35 per cent., Somerset 30 per cent. and Wiltshire 30 per cent. The enquiry also for the first time revealed publicly the vast possessions of individual landowners in the region. It showed that the Marquis of Bath, whose seat was at Longleat, owned 55,000 acres of which 20,000 were in Wiltshire and 8,000 in Somerset; that the Earl of Pembroke who lived at Wilton House owned 42,244 acres in Wiltshire, or some 5 per cent. of the whole county. The Duke of Beaufort at Badminton had an estate of 51,000 acres spread over the counties of Monmouth, Gloucester, Brecon, Glamorgan and Wiltshire; the Marquis of Lansdowne of Bowood Park possessed an estate of 142,916 acres, although much of this was in Scotland and Ireland. George Wingfield-Digby of Sherborne Castle owned 21,000 acres in Dorset and 5,000 in Somerset; the Earl of Ilchester who lived in the vast house at Melbury had 16,000 acres in Dorset, 13,000 acres in Somerset and 2,000 acres in Wiltshire; the Marquis of Ailesbury at Savernake had 55,000 acres which included 38,000 in Wiltshire. Many similar examples could be quoted, and such great estates, many of which had existed for many centuries, could hardly have failed to exercise a dominant role in the development of the landscape.

MEDIEVAL ESTATES

The effects of long centuries of domination by such great estates can be seen in landscape features and characteristics of all sorts. The medieval castles, those self-conscious symbols of royal and aristocratic power, survive in Dunster, Corfe Castle, Sherborne, Farleigh Hungerford, Longford near Salisbury and elsewhere. The ruins of many more are still to be seen or have been revealed by archaeological investigation: the great royal castles at Bristol and Bridgwater, for example, the Gurneys' stronghold at Richmont in the Chew valley south of Bristol, the Arundells' two great castles at Wardour (Wilts.) and Chideock (Dorset), the former great castles which dominated towns like Taunton, Marlborough, Devizes, Thornbury, Montacute or Trowbridge. In the later Middle Ages fortified strongholds like Nunney or Cothay or Woodsford, the former fortified and moated manor-house of the Abbots of Glastonbury at Ditcheat or perhaps the best example of all, the palace of the Bishops at Wells, gave way to more comfortable manor-houses like Barnston or Moigne Court in Dorset, Poundisford Park or Lytes Cary in Somerset, Great Chalfield, Westwood or South Wraxall in Wiltshire, or Sutton Court, Little Sodbury and Clevedon Court in Avon. There are scores of other examples in the region of such early manor-houses and of even larger establishments, including the greatest of all, Henry III's huge palace at Clarendon near Salisbury, of which scarcely anything now survives.

Other surviving features of the landscape also serve to remind of the medieval dominance of the region by a few great families. Deer-parks with their great earthen banks have left their imprint upon the landscape in many places and have affected the pattern of roads, the shapes of later fields and the place-names. They range in size from a few acres to nearly a thousand. Harbin's Park at Tarrant Gunville covers 115 acres and is still completely enclosed by a massive bank with an internal ditch, a prominent and evocative reminder of former land-use. The park surrounding the royal palace at Clarendon was more than three miles in diameter, while the bank along the south side of John of Gaunt's deer-park in King's Somborne is still 12 ft high. The bank and ditch which formerly surrounded the 145-acre deer-park of Milton Abbey is still remarkably well-preserved in the thick woodland of an isolated valley to the east of the former monastery. The carefully-constructed bank is still 3–4 ft high, and has remained intact even though the medieval town of Milton Abbey has disappeared from the landscape and the abbey has been transformed. The Bishops of Bath and Wells had deer-parks at several places in their diocese, including Bath, Ditcheat and Banwell; at the latter the boundary bank of the park was evidently surmounted by pales, for during the reign of Henry VII certain poachers were accused of having been hunting by night in the Bishop's park and of having killed 20 deer and set their heads on the park pales in defiance of the Bishop. The park banks and fences needed constant repair, and a thirteenth-century custumal of Glastonbury Abbey lists three days' work each year on the park fences at Pilton as one of the obligations of its tenants there. Such deer-parks were much more common than is often supposed, and wherever detailed local landscape or documentary investigation has been undertaken in the region, previously unknown deer-parks have been discovered. Other related landscape features which survive in many places include the remains of former rabbit warrens, fishponds and duck-decoys.

The great royal forests such as Selwood, Exmoor, Chippenham (or Pewsham), Braydon, Gillingham, Neroche and several others together with the huge area of Cranborne Chase, are another aspect of royal and aristocratic dominance of the medieval countryside. So also are the former royal hunting-palaces such as Gillingham and Tollard Royal where dramatic remains still exist, or Bagden Lodge in Savernake Forest near Marlborough and Grovely Lodge in Groveley Wood near Wilton. The royal forests continued as a dominant feature of the landscape until the seventeenth century. John Leland noted in 1540 the thick woodland of Melksham and Brayden 'Al the quarters of the foreste of Braden be welle woodid even along from Malmesbyri to Chippenham'. Saxton's map of 1567 and Speed's map of 1611 both show large areas of thickly wooded forest, and in the mid-seventeenth century Aubrey wrote that Melksham forest was 'full of goodly oakes, and so neer together that they say a squirrel might have leaped from tree to tree'. He added that a deer might have run in woodland all the way from Melksham to the Dorset coast. During the Civil War Clarendon Park still had 4,293 well-wooded acres.

TUDOR TO EARLY GEORGIAN

From the sixteenth century onward the number of gentry families increased greatly, as did also their concern for ever more comfortable and gracious houses, surrounded by parklands. Thomas Gerard, writing of Somerset and Dorset during the early seventeenth century, noted the increased prosperity of the yeomen and rich farmers who 'now beginne to encroach upon the Gentrie', and John Hooker, writing of Devon at the same time, was impressed by the number of new men 'clymbyng uppe daylely to the degree of Gentleman'. Of the 211 leading families of Dorset at the beginning of the seventeenth century, 103 or nearly half the total number had appeared for the first time in the ranks of the gentry during the previous century. At the same time the number of country houses and parks increased greatly with a correspondingly marked effect upon the landscape. There are so many examples of fine houses built in the region from the sixteenth century onwards that it is impossible to mention more than a very small proportion, and any selection must be inadequate. Some were enormous structures built in the latest styles, like Longleat, Montacute or Longford Castle; others were more modest, but nonetheless impressive, such as Chantmarle, the delightful house near Maiden Newton built by the Strode family with the date 1612 above the doorway, Newton Surmaville near Yeovil, Barrington near Ilminster, Avebury Manor in Wiltshire, or Winterbourne Anderson, the attractive house of soft-coloured red brick built by the Tregonwell family near Bere Regis in 1622. Scores of others were completely rebuilt or had extensions in the most modern style, such as Hinton St George, Brympton D'Evercy, Melbury House, Lulworth Castle, Kingston Lacy, and the new castle built by Sir Walter Raleigh at Sherborne close to the medieval castle which had belonged to the bishops of Salisbury. Smaller but nonetheless elegant houses of the later seventeenth century include the manor houses at Urchfont and Ramsbury in Wiltshire.

The Smyth family of Ashton Court just outside Bristol is a good example both of the way in which a 'new' gentry family could rise rapidly to wealth and prominence during the seventeenth century, and of their concern for their house and the surrounding parkland. John Smyth amassed a fortune as a Bristol merchant and bought Ashton Court together with a great deal of land in north Somerset and south Gloucestershire from the Arundel family in 1545. The house dated from the fifteenth century and consisted of a tower, a great hall, gallery, parlour, chapel, kitchen and several

60 Former duck decoy on Cheddar Moor, Somerset. Such decoys were once numerous. When filled with water the wild fowl which landed there were attracted into elaborately arranged nets by a specially trained dog (Photograph: J. E. Hancock)

chambers together with stable buildings, barns, gatehouse, dairy, brew-house and lodgings for the estate workmen. During the later sixteenth century John Smyth and his two sons were active in laying out a large deer-park around the house, stocking it with deer and planting it with trees. During the seventeenth century the family interest in their house and park continued and the surviving account books contain many references to expenditure on the park wall, on the deer and on the trees and gardens. Then in 1633 Thomas Smyth built a whole new wing on to the house. It was in a classical style, very advanced for its time, and was clearly intended to provide a visible reminder to all of the wealth and position to which the family had attained. Thomas Smyth's account book is full of references to the building work, to bringing stone from Dundry and from Bath, to paying workmen and masons, for timber and other building materials, and later to payment for laying out walks, gardens, a bowling green, and to the planting of trees and shrubs 'in the garden by the New Buyldinge'.

The laying out of extensive parkland around country houses was not always accomplished without affecting other people living in the neighbourhood or even other landowners. Sir Henry Baynton enclosed Spye Park near Calne during the early seventeenth century at the expense of the royal forest of Pewsham. He was also said to have killed the royal deer, felled the woods and built cottages in the forest which he let to his own tenants. His example obviously encouraged the royal keepers to neglect their duties and to kill the deer for their own use, for they were said to have

maytayned their whole houses and families on venison, and made it their ordinarie Meate, and gave theire servants noe other food.

Likewise in Selwood forest Sir John Thynne had carved out his park at Longleat from the surrounding thick woodland. The Duke of Somerset created a great new park at Savernake in spite of the protests of the tenants in surrounding manors who had traditionally enjoyed rights of feeding their cattle on the land; and the Herberts at Wilton likewise rode rough-shod over local objections when they made their great park. At Hinton St George successive extensions of their park by the Pouletts eventually destroyed the village of Hintonscroft, and at Orchardleigh near Frome the village disappeared beneath the carefully landscaped parkland of the Champneys family. In 1618 Mervyn Lord Audley, second Earl of Castle-haven purchased the manor of Stalbridge Dorset and began building a large house, now known as Stalbridge Park, to the north-west of the little town. The area surrounding Lord Audley's new mansion was 'a great pasture and waste and wooddy ground' which had been traditionally used as grazing-land by the tenants of Stalbridge manor. They not unnaturally objected very strongly to Lord Audley's high-handed methods and brought a case against him in the court of Chancery. They claimed that without their traditional grazing-rights on the great common they would be unable to maintain themselves or their families, nor would they be able to pay their rents to Lord Audley. The topographical evidence makes the result of this dispute quite clear. The tenants obviously lost their battle, for Lord Audley, who incidentally was later to achieve great notoriety and was eventually executed for a series of peculiarly bestial crimes including rape and sodomy, built his great house and enclosed the whole of the common with a great wall. This wall, especially solid and well-built, is more than five miles in length and more than six feet high; it still survives as one of the great Dorset monuments to aristocratic power and wealth, a reminder of R. H. Tawney's bitter remark on parks and parkland

made for those motives of social amenity and ostentation which have done so much to make the English countryside the admiration of travellers, and so much to ruin the English peasantry.

The great estates also affected the landscape in other ways. It was the great landowners who led the way in the drainage of marshlands and swamps, in the reclamation of forests and wastes, in the creation of water-meadows and in the introduction of new agricultural ideas and techniques. For example, the St John family of Lydiard Tregoze were responsible for draining and enclosing much of the heavy land in the north Wiltshire parishes of Hannington, Cricklade, Minety, Brokenborough and Purton during the seventeenth century. At Hannington the land before drainage was said to be 'lyinge in a deep watrye part of the cuntrye and subjecte often tymes to overflowinge with water and thereby to rott and hungerbane such sheep and cattle as were put to feede thereon'. Other land in the area was described as 'unprofitable, void and overgrown with brambles and briars, not worth twelvepence an acre'. After drainage with ditches and enclosure by pales and quick set hedges the land was said to be worth 13s 0d an acre. Much land in south Dorset was drained and improved at the instigation of Theophilus, Earl of Suffolk, the owner of Lulworth Castle and large estates in the surrounding area; and it was Henry Hastings, a younger son of the Earl of Huntingdon, who urged his tenants at Puddletown to go ahead with their plans for the construction of water-meadows in the valley there.

THE EIGHTEENTH CENTURY

The creation of ever-larger and more opulent houses and increasingly lavish parklands, gardens, lakes and woodlands continued throughout the eighteenth and nineteenth centuries. New sources of wealth and desire for grandeur created houses such as Dyrham Park or King's Weston near Bristol, Corsham Court, Ammerdown, Ston Easton, Bowood or the great mansion built at Eastbury near Tarrant Gunville, Dorset, for the famous eccentric George (Bubb) Doddington, an enormous masterpiece designed by Vanbrugh, of which little now survives. Often even more impressive than the houses themselves is the fact that parks and gardens grew ever larger and more elaborate, and the whole world was ransacked to provide new species of trees, new shrubs and new specimens of plants with which to decorate and adorn them. At Dyrham, Milton Abbas, Erlestoke, More Crichel and elsewhere whole villages were destroyed or were moved to other sites in order to lay out parks or to show off the mansion to best advantage. The work and influence of the great eighteenth-century landscape designers—William Kent (1685–1749), Lancelot (Capability) Brown (1715–83), Humphry Repton (1752–1818)—can be seen and felt throughout the region. William Kent's contribution to landscape gardening was to break away from the formal gardens which had surrounded seventeenth- and early eighteenth-century houses, and which can be seen, for example, in a view of Dyrham Park c. 1700, where the house is surrounded by elegant terraces, flower-beds and long lines of trees, all in straight lines disappearing into the distant perspective, in perfect symmetry and harmony. At Cranborne Manor the remains of the sevententh-century garden made up of nine regular beds each bounded by straight hedges of box and yew can still be seen. The great mansion at Eastbury built for Bubb Doddington between 1718 and 1738, had a formal garden laid out by Charles Bridgeman to a completely rectilinear design, with regular flower-beds, terraces and avenues, looking across the parkland dotted with square and triangular plantations of trees. Bridgeman had, however, invented the 'ha-ha' or sunken fence which served to keep animals out and yet gave the impression that the formal garden and the parkland beyond were all one. Although most of the mansion at Eastbury has gone, remains of Bridgeman's garden and landscaping survive.

It was William Kent who firmly established in the popular taste of land-owners during the eighteenth century the ideas of winding walks, irregular, serpentine stretches of water, waterfalls, grottoes, and eye-catching clumps of trees. Kent found the straight vistas, the regularly planted avenues and the formal box-edged flower-beds dull and uninspiring, and wished instead to create 'sudden changes of scene to ravish and surprise the beholders of temples, cascades, groves and statues in unexpected corners'. Kent's work can be seen in the lay-out of the grounds at Badminton, and possibly also in the superb gardens at Wilton. At Badminton, he was responsible for some of the decoration of the house, but above all for the park and its buildings, especially Worcester Lodge at the end of the three-mile ride with its ornamental gateways and with a gazebo on either side. In the same spirit are the Ragged Castle and other follies in the park at Badminton. Much more work in the region was, however, done by Capability Brown, who 'improved' the parklands. Capability Brown's work can be seen in the parklands at Wilton and Longleat, at King's Weston and Corsham Court and at Milton Abbey and Sherborne. Most notable of all, perhaps, is Brown's work at Bowood where he landscaped the grounds, created the grand vista along the lake, organised the massively extensive tree planting, and prepared the way for the Cascade, the Temple, the Grotto and the Mausoleum which were to add surprise and attraction to the scene.

Humphry Repton also worked extensively in the region. His work included laying out the park surrounding the Hippisley's grand new mansion at Ston Easton, complete with lake, gardens and carefully planted parkland vistas; completing the landscaping of the parks at Corsham Court and Longleat, both of which had been started by Brown; and, perhaps most notable and complete of all, the lay-out of the grounds at Blaise Castle near Bristol. At Blaise Castle can still be seen a splendid example of the self-consciously *picturesque* landscape, and this was completed by Repton's partner and collaborator John Nash (1752–1835) who designed the Orangery, the thatched Dairy and, above all, the ultimate expression of *picturesque* building, the romantic, rustic cottages of Blaise Castle hamlet.

The passion of the country gentry for fox hunting during the eighteenth and nineteenth centuries has also contributed to the development of the landscape. Many isolated pieces of woodland were planted and preserved as fox coverts, and many of the great houses of the region have elaborate stables and kennels. Without doubt the best example is at Badminton, where the splendidly appointed stables are built around all four sides of a large square courtyard, while beyond are the carefully designed kennels for the foxhounds. At Iwerne Steepleton what is now a row of cottages beside the main road through the village was originally built c. 1770 as kennels for the hounds of Peter Beckford, the enthusiastic Dorset fox-hunter and the author of a famous treatise on the subject, *Thoughts on Fox Hunting* first published in 1781.

But the two most spectacular examples of the way in which, given sufficient wealth, the whole landscape could be altered and moulded to suit new tastes have yet to be mentioned. The first is at Stourhead where Henry Hoare, a member of the wealthy family of bankers, began to lay out the grounds in the valley below his house in about 1741. During the following 30 years, landscaping, the creation of a lake, the planting of innumerable trees and shrubs, and the erection of bridges, temples, grottoes, and other buildings of all sorts, continued. The result is the most superb and remarkable example of landscape gardening in the whole region, and one of the most overwhelmingly beautiful pieces of artificial countryside ever created. It is the supreme example of the effect which a great estate and great wealth could have upon the landscape. The other example is William Beckford's extravaganza at Fonthill. Here at the end of the eighteenth century James Wyatt was employed to create a fantastic Gothic folly, a huge cruciform building 350 ft by 290 ft with, at the crossing, a great octagonal tower 225 ft high. Almost all of this is now gone, the tower itself collapsed in 1825 and most of the rest has been demolished, but the extravagant landscaping remains—the vast woodlands laid out by Beckford with, again, lakes, temples, grottoes, boat-houses, elaborate gateways and the other features created by that eccentric, wayward and extraordinarily wealthy genius.

Few places can match the size, magnificence or extravagance of Stourhead and Fonthill, but during the eighteenth and early nineteenth centuries the grounds of many country houses were graced with elaborate gateways, towers, monuments, grottoes and follies of all sorts. The finest of all these grottoes can be seen at Goldney House, built by Thomas Goldney with the date 1739 outlined in shells on the roof. The walls and roof of this large grotto are lined with shells, coral, 'Bristol diamonds' and other minerals, and it is provided with statues of lions and of the god Neptune and with an underground stream and pool, a superb example of the lengths to which eighteenth-century landscape gardeners and their wealthy patrons were prepared to go in order to achieve their exotic aims.

Many of the grottoes such as those at Fonthill, Bowood, Wardour, and perhaps Amesbury and Bowden Park, were constructed by Josiah Lane of Tisbury, who specialised in this work. Towers and obelisks embellish hill-tops all over the region—commemorating heroes, battles, landowners and other notable events. Follies in the form of sham castles, temples,

61 The Grotto at Goldney House, Clifton, Bristol, built
by Thomas Goldney in 1739 (Photograph: Gordon Kelsey)

ruined houses, elaborate gateways, lodges and triumphal arches, pavilions
and summer-houses are to be found adorning the parkland of countless
country houses. In Somerset alone, the larger hill-top monuments include
the Wellington obelisk on the Blackdown Hills, overlooking the town of
Wellington, erected to the Duke in 1817; the column erected at Burton-
Pysent by William Pitt in 1765 to commemorate his benefactor Sir William
Pysent, who left Pitt all his property both in Somerset and at Urchfont
in Wiltshire; the monument to Admiral Hood erected on the hill above
Butleigh in 1815; and the tower at Ammerdown erected in 1824 as a
memorial to Thomas Samuel Jolliffe who owned the estate and for whom
the fine house was built by James Wyatt. In Dorset, to mention only two
examples, the mansion at Wimborne St Giles is surrounded by a park
which includes a serpentine lake, splendid trees, a highly ornamented gateway, a temple, a fantastic grotto and a gazebo; Charborough park, also
well-wooded, has a grotto, a tall tower and four elaborate gateways, one surmounted by a deer, another by a lion and another by a stag. Just outside
the courtyard of Corsham Court is an elborate eighteenth-century folly
erected by the Methuen family, consisting of a tall artificial ruin evidently
intended to resemble a ruined church or monastery and to provide a view
from the windows of the house. All these things, like the multitude of other

154

such towers, follies, obelisks and extravagant gestures in stone are a further eloquent reminder of the power, wealth and influence of the gentry families, and of the control which they exercised over the landscape.

The influence of the gentry continued, and in some ways increased, during the nineteenth century. It was the great landowners who took the lead in securing enclosures and in promoting drainage schemes, especially the grandiose efforts which were made to drain the Somerset levels. The planting and management of woodlands continued, to supply timber, to provide coppice wood for the manufacture of hurdles, and for fox coverts and game preservation. The gentry were also to the fore in supporting schemes for road improvements, turnpikes, canals and in the building of railways, with all the indirect effects these had upon the countryside. It was the gentry and great landowners who pioneered the introduction of improved farming techniques, new crops, new implements, new methods and new breeds of livestock. It was men like John Billingsley (1747–1811) of Ashwick Grove near Shepton Mallet, who were in the forefront of all improvement schemes. Billingsley was himself a practical farmer, but he was also a member of the local Turnpike Trusts, he promoted the Somerset Coal Canal and the Kennet & Avon Canal, and he actively spread the work of the influential Bath & West Agricultural Society. It was Billingsley who was chosen by the newly-founded Board of Agriculture to write the *General View of the Agriculture of Somerset*, published in 1798. In this work Billingsley urged the necessity of improvements in farming practice, of enclosures, drainage and greater productivity, and his work was to have great influence during the next few decades. Similarly it was the Knight family on Exmoor who were responsible for turning more than 15,000 acres from worthless moorland into good agricultural land.

The work of such men is still very apparent in the landscape, in enclosed fields, drained lands and in rebuilt farm-houses and farm buildings. A good example is at East Harptree in the Chew Valley, south of Bristol. Much of the land in the parish belonged to the Gurney family of Harptree Court and, for want of male heirs, came into the possession of Miss Gurney who married the family butler, William Taylor. Taylor invested £15,000 of his wife's money in a spectacular model farm which was built at Eastwood Manor Farm during the years 1858–60. The farm consisted of 900 acres of land, and the model farmstead, which still survives and continues to be used for its original purpose, consisted of one and a quarter acres under a single roof. It was built of the latest materials with wide-span cast-iron pillars and arches, and is of two stories under a glass and galvanised-iron roof. All this survives entire. A nearby stream was used both to drive a water-wheel to provide power throughout the building, and also to sluice out the cattle-pens and bullocks' yard; the latter is also provided with a

62 Monument overlooking West Sedge Moor, Somerset, designed by 'Capability' Brown and erected by William Pitt in 1765 to the memory

fountain and drinking-trough. The lower floors provide cattle-housing and a milking-parlour, while the upper floor is used for grain and hay storage, all adapted to the latest farming methods. This exceptionally fine and inter-

of Sir William Pynsent who left his estate to Pitt as a tribute to his
success as Prime Minister (Photograph: J. H. Bettey)

esting building is a remarkable example of the impact which a single
wealthy family could have upon farming practice and upon the landscape
(*see* illustration **21** on page 42).

It was the great landowners who encouraged the planting of trees and the preservation of woodlands. The fact that so much of the region is well-wooded, adding immeasurably to its charm and beauty, is due very largely to the landowning gentry and to their passion for tree-planting. Their motives were various, and included a desire to beautify their surroundings, a concern for the landscape, a prudent care to have enough timber and coppice wood for the needs of their estates, and a realisation that timber was a good long-term investment. Other landowners were interested in the preservation of game and in providing suitable coverts for pheasants or for foxes. We cannot but be grateful to them and marvel at their energy and above all at the way in which they planted so much woodland as a decorative feature of their parklands, in the full knowledge that they would not live to see the fully developed results of their initiative. The effect of their endeavours is still apparent over the many well-wooded areas of the region.

Tree planting was encouraged by landlords from the Middle Ages onwards, and many manorial customs laid down that the tenants should plant trees each year, as for example at Brigmerston and Milston near Amesbury, where it was ordered by the manorial court in 1611,

that everye tennant of this mannor shall for every yarde lande att seasonable tyme sett one timber tree of oake, ashe and elme and one fruite tree, and shall from tyme to tyme Cherishe and nourishe them.

In the nineteenth century clumps of woodland were planted on the downland above Amesbury to represent the positions occupied by the main ships in the English and French fleets at a significant stage in the Battle of Trafalgar. All over the downland less dramatic evidence of tree-planting by great landowners and great estates survives in the form of the beech plantations created as windbreaks on exposed crests of the downs. Fine examples of groups of trees, now prominent features of the landscape, which were originally planted as windbreaks, can also be seen at the aptly-named Windwhistle on the exposed hill-top in south Somerset between Crewkerne and Chard; and at Holford beeches on the Quantocks. Such plantings were strongly urged by agricultural writers and reformers of the eighteenth and nineteenth centuries. For example John Billingsley, a leading exponent of improved farming methods in Somerset during the Napoleonic Wars wrote that

Judicious and well-disposed belts and clumps of trees increase the beauty as well as the value of new inclosures. There are very few descriptions of soil or climate where trees of some kind will not grow in clumps. They afford shelter and defence to the fields, are pleasant to the eye and ultimately profitable.

It was also the enthusiasm of the gentry families for tree-planting that introduced so many new varieties of trees and shrubs during the eighteenth and nineteenth centuries. The number of trees planted was prodigious. At Bowood during the late eighteenth century the Earl of Shelburne planted 150,000 trees each year. At Stourhead during the 1790s Colt Hoare planted more than 2,000 acres of woodland; his surviving account books show payments for beech, chestnut, ash, birch, elm, holly, oak, sycamore, maple and thorn. He also introduced the rhododendron, probably the ancestors of those which now cover the borders of the lake. During the nineteenth century a range of new varieties were introduced to Stourhead including the big Californian Redwoods, Western Red Cedar, Monterey and Lawson Cypresses and many shrubs. At Fonthill during the 1790s William Beckford was also engaged in tree-planting on a massive scale in the extensive grounds surrounding his vast and eccentric 'Abbey', using trees and shrubs of all kinds, but preferring indigenous species such as oak, birch, Scotch fir and larch.

But it was not only the extremely wealthy landowners who were interested in tree-planting. On a much more modest estate than those already mentioned, two landowners who were passionately devoted to their woodlands, both as a commercial venture and as an adornment to their estate, were James Frampton of Moreton in Dorset and his son, also James. During the period of the Napoleonic Wars they planted many thousands of trees and completely transformed the appearance of that part of Dorset. Their detailed estate diaries and accounts show that between 1791 and 1800 for example, no less than 600,000 trees were planted on their estate, and the work continued at a similar rate during the following decades, 104,878 trees being planted in 1815, and the highest number of all, 153,616 in 1817. Most of these were timber trees or were destined to provide posts and fencing on the estate such as Scotch Fir, Beech, Oak, Chesnut, Spruce and Larch. The effect upon the landscape of that part of Dorset of such enormous plantings was immense and it is to men like the Framptons and many other similarly-minded country gentlemen that we owe many of the hardwood plantations.

In Somerset the growing of willows to provide withies has had a marked influence on the appearance of the low-lying lands where the drainage channels or rhynes are fringed with ancient willows, each carefully pollarded so that the new shoots to provide the withies grow high up out of reach of browsing cattle. Elsewhere in the county the large number of cider-apple orchards, and the practice of growing hedgerow trees—especially elm—for timber and to provide fencing poles, gave even districts which were largely devoted to arable farming a wooded character.

During the twentieth century the part once played by the great landowners in tree-planting has been taken over by the Forestry Commission. Through their efforts many thousands of acres in the Dorset heathlands which had previously been derelict and unproductive have been planted with conifers, while large areas of woodland have been planted on the Quantocks, Exmoor and the Brendons. On Mendip more than 1,500 acres of mixed woodlands are managed by the Forestry Commission.

Recent years have seen the sorry spectacle of large areas of the region almost denuded of trees by Dutch elm disease. The elm was by far the commonest hedgerow tree over large parts of Somerset, north Wiltshire and west Dorset, and the total loss of these splendid trees has been a tragedy for the appearance of the landscape.

ESTATE VILLAGES AND COUNTRY HOUSES

The work of gentry families during the nineteenth century can also be seen in many other features of the landscape, in the building of model cottages, schools, almshouses, hospitals and other public buildings, and also in the multitude of new or restored churches, a majority of which owed their origin or their restoration to the initiative and support of local gentry. The work of building great country houses also went on through the nineteenth century, and the results can be seen in such mansions as Orchardleigh near Frome, Hestercombe near Taunton, Rood Ashton near Trowbridge, Tottenham House near Marlborough and many others. Perhaps the aggressive use of wealth and the total assurance of aristocratic power can best be seen in one of the last of the great country houses to be erected, Lord Portman's house at Bryanston. It was designed by Norman Shaw and built during the 1890s; its stark, uncompromising outline, emphasised by the bright red of its brickwork, dominates the town of Blandford Forum from its position on a hill-top overlooking the town.

It would be wrong to suggest that the gentry families were always successful, that they were no more subject to failure and disaster than other mortals or that their houses were no more liable to change and decay. Although there are many notable exceptions, a large number of gentry and landowning families prominent in the sixteenth and seventeenth centuries no longer exist, and few parishes are without the ruins of at least one former gentry house. This is no new phenomenon. William Cobbett in his Rural Rides down the valley of the Avon in Wiltshire towards Salisbury in 1826 noted the disappearance or ruin of many former manor-houses. He estimated that in a distance of 30 miles down the valley there were formerly 50 mansions, of which only eight survived.

There are many of the mansion-houses the ruins of which you yet behold. At Milton there are two mansion-houses, the walls and the roofs of which yet remain, but which are falling gradually to pieces, and the garden walls are crumbling down. At Enford, Bennet, the member for the county, had a large mansion-house, the stables of which are yet standing. In several places I saw, still remaining, indubitable traces of an ancient manor-house, namely a dove-cote or pigeon house. The poor pigeons have kept possession of their heritage, from generation to generation, and so have the rooks, in their several rookeries, while

63 The church and almshouses on the estate of the
Earls of Shaftesbury at Wimborne St Giles (Photograph: J. H. Bettey)

the paper-system has swept away, or rather swallowed-up, the owners of the
dove-cotes and of the lofty trees....

We can end this chapter with the story of one such ruined house and of
the gentry family who built it and whose effect upon the surrounding landscape is still clearly to be seen. The family were the Pophams who
flourished from the reign of Elizabeth I until the twentieth century, and
who possessed, besides the great house and estate at Littlecote in Wiltshire,
extensive properties around Houndstreet (now known as Hunstrete) in the
parish of Marksbury, five miles south-west of Bath. Their influence on
the landscape can be seen in all the surrounding villages which were formerly part of the Popham estates and where all the houses and farms are
unmistakably built in the same 'estate' style, and all bear a large letter 'P'
as further evidence of their origin and ownership. The family house at
Houndstreet was a building of the sixteenth and early seventeenth centuries set in wooded parkland. In the 1770s Francis Popham, who then
owned the estate, decided to build a large new mansion on the site on a
grand scale. The new house was built of Bath stone and had a front of
seventeen bays. It included elaborate plaster-work, statues, carvings and

decoration. Large-scale gardens were laid out, a long sweeping carriage-drive made, and landscaping work in the surrounding parkland involved the planting of many hundreds of trees, several long avenues, and the creation of a chain of six lakes across which the new house looked. Stable-blocks, carriage-houses and other outbuildings were erected and a large ice-house was made, dug deep into a nearby hillside. Francis Popham died in 1779 long before his vast project was complete, but the work was energetically continued by his widow Dorothy until her death in 1797, by which time most of the house was complete. They had no children and so all the properties passed to a relative, General Leyborne Popham, who lived at the family's other mansion, Littlecote in Wiltshire. The great house at Houndstreet therefore lay empty and unused, and deteriorated rapidly. The Rev. John Skinner, the antiquarian and archaeologist, who was rector of nearby Camerton, visited Houndstreet in 1822 to picnic by the lakes, and wrote that

Although upwards of thirty thousand pounds were expended on the Mansion and Grounds not many year since, the whole is fast going to decay ... the noble piece of water is covered with weeds and long grass; thistles and nettles cover the walks....

By 1831 the house was in such a bad state that General Popham decided to demolish it. Some of the materials, including sculptures, were sold to Prior Park, Bath, and used for alterations carried out there after a fire in 1836. Today the lakes and the landscaping survives, the avenues and plantations are still the most prominent feature of the surrounding area, the ice-house still exists in a bank near the site of the house, but of the house itself only a few pillars which once fronted the drawing-room windows stand in the middle of a grass field, as a reminder of the great mansion that once stood there and as a dramatic illustration of how quickly and completely such a symbol of wealth and power can disappear from the landscape.

Bibliography

M. ASTON & T. ROWLEY. *Landscape Archaeology* (1974)

M. ASTON & J. BOND. *The Landscape of Towns* (1976)

R. ATTHILL. *Old Mendip* (1964)

R. ATTHILL (ed.). *Mendip, A New Study* (1976)

R. H. BAKER & J. B. HARLEY. *Man Made the Land* (1973)

R. S. BARRON. *The Geology of Wiltshire* (1976)

J. H. BETTEY. *Dorset* (1974)
    Rural Life in Wessex (1977)

H. C. BOWEN. *Ancient Fields* (1961)

A. BUCHANAN & N. COSSONS. *Industrial Archaeology of the Bristol Region* (1969)

M. C. CORFIELD (ed). *A Guide to the Industrial Archaeology of Wiltshire* (1978)

O. G. S. CRAWFORD. *Archaeology in the Field* (1953)

H. C. DARBY & R. W. FINN *The Domesday Geography of South-West England* (1976)

H. C. DARBY (ed.). *A New Historical Geography of England* (1973)

G. DARLEY. *Villages of Vision* (1975)

R. W. DUNNING (ed.). *Christianity in Somerset* (1976)

R. W. DUNNING. *A History of Somerset* (1978)

P. FOWLER. *Regional Archaeologies: Wessex* (1976)

M. GELLING. *Signposts to the Past* (1978)

L. V. GRINSELL. *The Archaeology of Wessex* (1958)

G. HADFIELD. *The Canals of South West England* (1967)

W. G. HOSKINS. *The Making of the English Landscape* (1953)
    Fieldwork in Local History (1967)
    Local History in England (1968)

J. S. MOORE (ed.). *Avon Local History Handbook* (1979)

N. PEVSNER *The Buildings of England series*, various

K. PONTING *Churches of Wessex* (1977)

T. ROWLEY *Villages in the Landscape* (1978)

C. TAYLOR *The Making of the English Landscape: Dorset* (1970)
    Fieldwork in Medieval Archaeology (1974)
    Fields in the English Landscape (1975)

R. WHITLOCK *Historic Forests of England* (1979)

M. WILLIAMS *The Draining of the Somerset Levels* (1970)

List of Illustrations

Index

References in italics are to the page numbers of illustrations